'My heart overflows with a good theme;
I address my verses to the King:
My tongue is the pen of a ready writer.'
Psalm 45:1

First Printing 2018
Printed in the United Kingdom by Create Space
Copyright © 2018 by Anna E Honeysett

Editor: E. Verlinden
Design for cover and typesetting: Doodle my Domain (www.doodlemydomain.co.uk)

ISBN- 978-1-9164961-0-1

www.honeysettcounselling.co.uk

Although the author and publisher have made every effort to ensure that the information
in this book was correct at press time, the author and publisher do not assume and
hereby disclaim any liability to any party for any loss, damage, or disruption caused by
errors or omissions, whether such errors or omissions result from negligence, accident, or
any other cause. Please be aware that all of the advice and guidance is written from the
author's experience and point of view and they cannot guarantee the same outcomes
they have experienced.

How to set up a successful counselling practice

Anna Honeysett

Acknowledgements

As a little girl I didn't have much self confidence when it came to learning. I used to look around and wonder why my peers seemed to read and write with such ease. As someone who suffers from dyslexia I was often told 'you're not academic but creative' or 'don't worry Anna you will be brilliant at a practical job.' After a while these words bedded in and I accepted that I just wasn't that intelligent.

So to be sitting here today writing the acknowledgements for my book is more than a surprise but a small miracle. I never dreamt that I would have the vision or discipline to sit down and write thousands of words in my spare time and yet here I am!

Of course I needed some help along the way and there are some very special people I would like to thank. Firstly I would like to thank God, Father you are where all my inspiration and strength comes from and I could not have done this without your loving presence in my life. Ellie - I adore your brilliant brain and servant heart. Your attention to detail is a real gift and one that has blessed me so much through this journey - thank you! Debbie - Your creativity and meticulous work inspires me to do things better. I could not have been blessed with a more helpful and encouraging friend, thank you for putting up with my frustrations and self doubt. I will pay you in cereal! Trish - Thank you for your willingness to help and excellent proofreading skills. Your love of prawn sandwiches still makes me smile. Thank you to all my wonderful friends and family that have taken an interest and encouraged me through this venture. Finally thank you to my mum and dad for always being there no matter what life brings.

Over the last few years I have learned that not only do I have something important to say, I am an intelligent, resilient woman who isn't afraid of hard work. If there is something in your life that you have been told you cannot achieve or are 'not good enough' to do then please do yourself a favour and rewrite your script.

I am living proof that if you put your mind to something then despite your self doubt you can achieve it.

Dream big! Anna x

Author biography

Anna has worked in the therapeutic field for the last fifteen years and has extensive knowledge and experience in group work, one to one counselling and training.

After setting up her own very successful counselling practice she discovered a passion for business and helping others reach their potential in this area.

She lives in Ashford, Kent and in her spare time enjoys baking, mini adventures and spending time with friends and family including her cat Suki.

Anna Honeysett

Contents

Introduction

Hello and welcome. If you have purchased this book then it is likely that you or someone you know is thinking about setting up a therapy business and you need some guidance on where to start.

I was inspired to write this book because as I went through my own journey of setting up in private practice I found there were very limited resources out there to help our specific profession. As someone who has 'been there and done it' I felt it would be encouraging to share with you my tips and findings along the way and save you some time having to figure it all out yourself.

Firstly who is this book for? Well it is for counsellors, psychotherapists and psychologists who are looking to set up their own private practice. A lot of the information I am going to share can be used for starting any business. However as a therapist I found that there are certain aspects of our role that require more than just a straightforward business model.

Setting up a business can feel really scary and although you feel ready as a therapist you may feel overwhelmed by the idea of becoming a business person. My aim is to break the process down for you into bite- size pieces so you can approach your setup with ease and order. I have also tried to write each chapter in the order you will need to do things to make it more accessible (although obviously you can still dip in and out of the book as you need.)

In regards to making notes I have intentionally created a notes section at the end of each chapter. This is only applicable if you have a hard copy of the book so for all you lovely ebook buyers out there I would suggest that you keep a journal or take some notes as you go along so you don't forget your brilliant ideas.

There is also a practical checklist at the end of each chapter to help you stay on top of every step you need to take.

I really hope this book is a gift to you and makes your journey into private practice an enjoyable one. Please feel free to review my book online through amazon.

Right, introduction done let's crack on with the first chapter.

Getting inspired and doing your research

At some point something will have inspired you to start thinking about private practice. Maybe you're fresh out of training and you are ready to spread your wings and grow in your skills. Maybe you have been volunteering and now would like to be paid for what you do, or maybe like me you have always had a desire to do what you love to do and make a successful living out of it. Whatever route you are coming into private practice from, something will have sparked a fire in you and it is important to recognise what it is. I say this because although it is very achievable to create a successful business, it will require tenacity and hard work to reach your goal and knowing why you started this process will help you if things get tough. Here are some helpful questions to ask yourself before we move on.

Why do I want to be in private practice?
Am I ready for private practice?
As a therapist what am I passionate about?
What will push me forward if things get tricky?

I just want to pay attention to one of the questions on this list and that is 'Am I ready for private practice?.' My answer to this question would be what do *you* think? Only you know the answer to this. For some people they really do need more training or experience working within an organisational setting, for others like myself I already had ten years of therapeutic work behind me and I was chomping at the bit to get started. There is no fixed answer or ideal amount of hours so don't look for one from others but look inwardly at yourself - you will know what and when is right for you.

Upfront costs of setting up your practice

As with setting up any business there are always going to be upfront costs and I think it is always advisable to budget slightly higher than what you anticipate so you don't get any nasty surprises! I had very little money when I started so I concentrated on the aspects of my business that would be essential. This was my website and paying for someone to create something excellent, business cards, being registered on a therapist directory, a decent and accessible room and supportive regular supervision. There are also one off yearly payments that you may be paying already such as membership fees, training, insurance and being registered with the ICO. (I cover all of these aspects in detail later on)

Just remember as you accumulate clients you will be able to purchase more for your practice. If you don't have much money to play with initially then pace yourself and accept you may not be able to have everything you want all at once (I know it's hard!)

What is encouraging is a lot of what I share in this book will not cost you anything in money but more in time and effort and will still ensure wonderful results.

Research

Once I had decided that I wanted to work in private practice I knew I had to do some research about how to go about this. What do I mean by research? I like this clear definition from Merriam-Webbster Dictionary (1828) 'A careful or diligent search...the collecting of information about a particular subject.'

To get started for my research I did a search of who was working in my area. Counselling directories and membership body directories are great for getting a sense of who is operating near to you and what they are offering. I did this for two reasons:

1. Like it or not they are your competition.

2. They are your peers and will be an important network for you especially when you get super busy and need to refer clients on.

An example of research that I undertook was when deciding on what my company was going to be called. I had about four different options and so I sent these options to close friends and family to see what they thought. My findings were pretty unanimous with the odd random offering and I was happy with the result.

Advice from others is great and definitely helpful but it is always good to weigh it up with what you think and if you are confident about your decision then go with it, It is your business after all.

Specialisms

At this early stage I was starting to work out what my specialisms were and how I was different from other therapists. Having worked with addictions and eating disorders this was something I knew I could offer.

If you have an area of expertise then use it to your advantage. Start thinking about what yours are and what is going to separate you from the pack.

Your company name

Choosing a company name was one of the most exciting tasks in the beginning. It is a real chance to get your creative juices flowing so it's ok to get excited about it. This name is going follow you and it is your first step to branding your business. I chose to use my surname because I like it (people compliment me on it quite a lot!) and I wanted my name to be the face of my company. Personal names are great, but be wary of using your first name in case you expand in the future and clients expect to see you and not an associate.

Having the word 'counselling', 'psychotherapy' or 'psychology' in your name is also a good idea because when you create your website having what you offer in the title is going to significantly increase your chances of being found online. (we will cover this in chapter four.)

Don't be too abstract as you want your name to sound professional and be easy to find. I have noticed that there are a lot of names that include trees, pebbles or other natural ideas. Again this is fine (I have a bee in my logo); however it is also about being a bit different and not blending in with other therapists. Do your research and see what else is out there because you don't want to be in a position where you name your company and then find there is someone with the same or very similar name. What's great is when you go to buy your domain name the site does show you if someone else has a similar name to what you are after. If this is the case I would suggest coming up with another idea.

Using your contacts

Finally, the greatest advice I was given at the very start of my journey, was to make a list of all the people I knew who may have skills or experience that could help with setting up my business. For example when thinking about my company logo I remembered I had a friend who was a graphic designer and she offered to do my logo for a fraction of the price in exchange for her using it for her online portfolio. I also have a great friend who is very computer literate so I spent time with her learning how to use programmes on the computer that I didn't know how to use. Be creative and don't ever be afraid to ask. I am not suggesting that you take advantage but in my experience people are often so willing to help.

To conclude, something else I did for research purposes was to meet with someone who I knew was already running a successful counselling business. Not only will you learn tips from them you will also hopefully feel encouraged that you CAN do the same.

Anna's Answers

- Ask yourself *why* you are going into private practice and what is going to motivate you if things get tough?
- Do a rough budget for setting up costs.
- Start by doing some simple research on what the competition is like in your area and what other therapists are offering.
- What are your specialisms? How can you use them to your advantage?
- Don't be afraid to utilise the contacts you already have, people are often willing to help, so ask.
- Finally, meet up with another therapist who is already doing well in private practice so you can learn from them and be encouraged.

Check List

- ❏ Researched other therapists in my area and what they are offering
- ❏ Do a rough budget for set up costs (thinking about just the essentials)
- ❏ Think about what my specialisms are
- ❏ Choose a business name
- ❏ Write a list of all the people who can help me with my business and contact them
- ❏ Contact and meet another therapist who is already running a successful private practice

Notes:

....
....
....
....
....
....
....
....
....
....
....
....
....
....
....
....
....
....
....
....
....
....
....
....

Chapter Two

Building foundations

This chapter is exactly what it says on the tin, it's time to start building your business' foundations. Now I warn you some of these aspects are really quite dull (well I found them dull) but are super important nonetheless. Hopefully by now you will have chosen your company name, seen who is available to support you in your journey and done some basic research of your area.

Sole Trader or Limited Company

There are two options for your business either you can become a sole trader or you can create a limited company. When I spoke to other therapists they suggested setting up as a sole trader as it is a cheaper option and slightly simpler. In order to set up a limited company you have to pay and it may take more effort administratively when it comes to tax returns, whereas being a sole trader is free.

On the flip side being a limited company means that you are not linked personally to any of the company finances i.e you are 'limited' by shares. This means your company has its own legal identity. For some people if they are investing a lot of money or borrowing money it can feel reassuring to know that whatever happens with their business their family assets are not at risk.

When thinking about employing others you can still do this as a sole trader, you just need to make sure that you are collecting income tax and national insurance from them. You can do this by setting up a PAYE (Pay as you earn) payroll scheme, which is available on the HMRC website. This really is a personal choice and you can change your status along the way (which I will do in due course when I grow considerably and my overheads are higher, therefore I'm more at risk)

HMRC

Once you have done this it is important to register your business with HMRC. This is so you are registered as an official business and enables you to pay your taxes. You can do this online at https://www.gov.uk/log-in-register-hmrc-online-services and follow the links for registering a new business. They will then send you confirmation through the post in a couple of weeks. Keep this for your records.

Bank Accounts

Once your company is registered you can set up a bank account for your business. A lot of people ask 'Do I need to have a business account can I not just open another regular account?' My advice would be yes you need a business account as you want all of your finances to be transparent. You can be accused of money laundering and other financial offences more easily if you are using a personal account for business purposes. You will find that most banks offer at least two years of free depositing so you won't be charged for having a business account for quite some time and even when you are, the cost is minimal and tax deductible.

I chose to open mine at my current bank so that when paying myself a wage and wanting to transfer money between accounts it would be easier. (mobile banking has changed my life for this!) It also means that if you want clients to pay you via BACS transfer you are giving them a proper business account to pay into; you want to keep all your personal and business finances separate.

I was advised to open a savings account linked to Honeysett Counselling so that each month I could transfer across money for tax. In order to complete this process pop into your chosen bank and explain what you need and they will arrange an appointment for you to open the accounts and explain how it all works. Mine were very helpful and I found the process pretty painless.

You will need to consider how you are going to keep your financial records but we will explore this in much more depth in chapter six so more on that later.

Insurance

Next on the agenda is indemnity insurance to cover you for any mishaps in the workplace or if a client makes a complaint against you. It is very important that you protect yourself as an individual particularly as a sole trader. As a student I was happy with the insurance company I was with, I just needed to upgrade from student to qualified practitioner. If you are in the same position, then all you need to do is give your current insurer a call and they will then ask you to send them a copy of your qualification via email and then pay the difference. If you haven't had to have insurance recently then do not worry the process is the same, they will still want proof of your credentials and then take a payment over the phone. You will then receive a copy of your insurance certificate in the post, again keep this in a safe place for your records. The most common companies that insure therapists are Holistic, Towergate and Howden, so shop around and see what deals they can offer you.

How much you insure for is up to you, I am covered for £10,000,000 overall which covers you for malpractice and professional liability, public liability and product liability. It is vital to remember that your insurance only covers you for your chosen modality so think about the way you advertise; as stating something that you do not actually have a professional qualification for will invalidate your insurance.

Disclosure Barring Service (DBS)

As you are working with members of the public particularly those that are vulnerable or minors, it is really important for you to hold a recent DBS. If you are already working in an organisation that requires one, as long as it is in date this should cover you. If not, you will need to acquire one for your company. This is a bit more tricky as you cannot obtain one as an individual. What you need to do is find what's called a DBS umbrella body company. You can search for companies that can to do a criminal record check on behalf of your business. To do this visit GOV.UK and they will guide you through the process. Note you will have to visit the umbrella body company in person to show them your relevant documents.

It is also advisable that you sign up to their yearly renewal service which means that you can transfer your DBS to other organisations, update, add and remove certificates.

Membership Bodies

Finally you need to think about which membership body you are going to be registered with if you're not already. Since I completed a British association for counsellors and psychotherapists (BACP) accredited course it made sense for me to continue with them. The process is simple you just need to call them to register as a qualified member. You'll be asked to send through your certificate of your diploma or degree and your indemnity insurance as well. They will then register you on the system. Again there will be a charge of some kind if you are converting from your student status. If not you will already be paying full rate and hopefully will already be a registered member. The BACP now ask that you complete their register online which is very quick and easy but it is important you do this so they have all the correct information. Other membership bodies are available The National Counselling Service (NCS) are becoming more popular, the UK Council for Psychotherapists (UKCP) and the Health and Care Professional council (HCPC)

Membership for any body costs money and you may ask 'Do I really need to be registered with one?' Well there is no law saying so, in the same way currently anyone can call themselves a counsellor; however if you want to practice in a safe and ethical way it would be a very good idea. Just like your insurance, they are there to protect and advise you and it means there is a greater organisation outside of you and your supervisor. I like that they keep me accountable in a fast changing profession. It also gives my clients reassurance. Furthermore, most advertisers and organisations require you to adhere to a membership body just like many other professions. With most membership bodies you also get access to online events and training and a monthly magazine. To help you with the cost they allow you to spread the cost over the year, which is great if you are starting out and low on funds.

Anna's Answers

- I know that some of these tasks are a bit boring but spend the time as they really are the supporting layers to your company.
- Think about your decision to be a sole trader or a limited company. The long term direction of your business will be the best way to determine this.
- Remember to register your company online with HMRC.
- Make an appointment with your bank to open your business account and savings account for your tax.
- Look at your insurance and make sure that you update all of your details so that you are covered for the next year.
- Think about how you are going to acquire a DBS and take relevant action.
- Finally make sure you join or upgrade with a reputable membership body.

Practical checklist

- ❏ Decide between becoming a sole trader or a limited company
- ❏ Go online and register my business with the HMRC and store information securely
- ❏ Arrange a business bank account and savings account for tax
- ❏ Update or buy my indemnity insurance and store information securely

- ❏ Update my DBS or find an umbrella company local to me
- ❏ Update or register with a reputable membership body

Well done! You have achieved a lot so far, on to Chapter Three.

Notes:

....
....
....
....
....
....
....
....
....
....
....
....
....
....
....
....
....
....
....
....
....
....
....
....

Chapter Three

Finding yourself a great space

This section is going to be split in two as we have a lot to get through and I don't want you to feel overloaded. The first part is about how to pick a suitable place to work from and the sort of questions you need to consider. The second part is more about your room environment and how to create a positive, beautiful space in which to work in, for you and your clients.

Part One

Where will you be based

As I live in Ashford it made sense to me that this was where I was going to practice. Now is the time to think about where is going to be most accessible for you and your clients. It may be helpful when doing your research to see how many therapists are in your area and if it is oversaturated thinking about alternatives.

You may have decided to work from home and we will look at the pro and cons of home working later.

I found my first counselling location about a month before I had even qualified. I was visiting a friend's chiropractor business and I was sat in their waiting room. It was peaceful, bright and they had a great coffee machine (very important in my opinion). As I was sitting there waiting for my appointment it struck me that I could really see myself working there. As I ruminated on this during my appointment my friend asked me what I planned to do when I qualified. It was quite funny really, there I was with my face squashed in a hole of the plinth, being leant upon with great force and me trying to explain my upcoming business plans! However, it was then that he said, "well when you qualify give me a call and we will see what we can do." Although this is not my main room now, I still see clients out of their premises and thoroughly enjoy my time there.

Choosing a room

In private practice you can become very isolated and so choosing to operate out of an already established business is only going to help you. You can rent a room in an office block or hall but it's being aware that there will be very little sense of team or ready made connections. I have found that being based in a chiropractic clinic also brings in new clients because my friend happily makes referrals and lets me put out leaflets and business cards in their waiting room. Have a look in your area at chiropractors, osteopaths, massage therapists, nutritionists and other holistic clinics. They often rent rooms at an hourly or daily rate.

How much should I pay

When you rent a room you need to consider how much you are willing to pay and adjust your hourly rate accordingly so you make enough profit. I have found that it all depends on the area. Typically you can pay anything between five pounds to thirty pounds per client. The other option is to book the room for a block booking so that you are paying for a day or an afternoon. I have found that if you can pay per client then this is the best way to limit costs but if you find a better deal then of course go with that.

Room agreement and insurance

The place you have chosen to work from may already have a room agreement so you need to go over that with a fine tooth-comb and make sure you are happy with what they are proposing.

Good questions to ask are:

- What hours are available?
- Do you rent your room on a daily/half day rate?
- What does my room rate cover? Internet, electricity, heating, seating, tissues, water, tea/coffee etc
- Is it in a quiet location in the building?
- Is there a toilet available?
- Do I still pay for the room if my client does not attend?
- When and how can I access the room?
- How much notice do I need to cancel my booking?
- Is there anywhere I can store belongings? (e.g. a locked cupboard for sand trays, pens, pencils spare items)
- Will other people be using the building?
- How often will I be working on my own there?
- Who cleans and maintains the room? (should be owner)

If they do not have a room agreement, don't be afraid to either ask for one or draft one up yourself.

If they have a receptionist, it's also important to consider whether you wish to use their booking system or arrange appointments with your clients independently. I prefer self management, you have more control over your diary and they may also charge extra to use their secretarial services. However, as your practice grows you may feel differently about this.

It is also important to make sure the building or organisation has the right insurance themselves and that they are allowed to sublet a room under their contract.

As someone who suffers from a chronic bowel condition I am quite passionate about people's right to accessible toilet facilities! It is helpful to remember when clients come to therapy they may feel very nervous and need the comfort of a loo close by. I have also experienced clients telling me that they have felt sick or needed to use a toilet urgently after sessions, because often the bodies response to emotional stress is to evacuate all waste. So, when looking around at possible premises bear this in mind. If you are working from home I suggest letting your client know where the toilet is. Mine is upstairs (I very rarely have clients at home now) but to ensure my privacy I shut all doors leading to other rooms.

Having a similar outlook to your premises

One of the things that struck me when wanting to work out of the chiropractic clinic was the lovely atmosphere. I very much agree with what they are offering and so this helps to have a positive relationship with the other staff members that are working there. When you go and visit a potential room, ask yourself: 'Do I like it here?' 'Is it a nice calm environment?' 'If I was a client would I want to come here?' Always go with your gut instinct. You may get a great deal but not a very nice environment. Remember first impressions count and you want people to remember you for good reasons not because you were working out of a dodgy building!

Lone working and assessing risk

Lone working is something as therapists we need to consider. If you have chosen a space then it's really important you do a good risk assessment. You need to be aware of who is in the building, and what you would do if there was an emergency or you were at risk of harm. Some places have panic buttons but it's rare in my experience.

Little things can go a long way, such as letting someone know what time and where you are seeing a client. If the building you have chosen has a receptionist it can be a good idea to give them a list of your client times, so they are aware of your schedule and keep an ear out for your safety.

However there may be times where nobody else is around and that's life, we can't have the ideal situation all of the time. With risk it is all about using your common sense and making sure that you feel safe and if you don't then please don't compromise yours or your client's safety, it just isn't worth it.

My advice would be to **never** assess a new client when you are on your own. Your first meeting will tell you a lot and it will help you assess risk with this person. After that if you can follow the steps above then it is advisable.

Access to your location
Parking and disabled access is really important. If you are in a really inaccessible area then this may put potential clients off and ultimately result in them not choosing you. If you are working in a busy town or city think about where the nearest parking is, where the bus routes are and how near a drop off point is to your chosen location. Remember not everyone drives so having a place that can be accessed by public transport is vital.

The same considerations apply to inside the premises. Think about the stairs, whether the corridors are wide enough for wheelchair access and if there are disabled toilets or facilities big enough to accomodate people with mobility difficulties. I would suggest thinking about room size as well, not just for access reasons but for general comfort. When I was doing my training placement I was offered the smallest room possible in a health centre. The window was tiny and barely opened, not to mention the fact I was working for a bariatric service so the clients who were coming really struggled to get in the door and comfortably get to their seats. I found the room suffocating and so did my clients. I felt it also added to the shame that they were already feeling about their size. Now working in private practice I make sure all of these bases are covered for the benefit of me and my clients.

Travel costs

When you start setting up a business you will probably notice yourself thinking about how you can save on the small things. Good questions to ask are 'How far away is my clinic?' 'How much money on travel will I be spending?' 'Do I need to pay for parking?'

I have two different locations and I can walk to one and drive to the other. This is great as it means I'm spending much less on fuel, which keep my profits reasonable. Unfortunately you can no longer claim mileage to and from work so it is worth considering how much you will be spending on fuel and car costs.

Working from home

Many therapists choose this option and it is a good one but I just want to raise a few points to help you consider if this is the right choice for you.

Firstly, 'How do you feel about having clients in your home?' Remember this is your space so you need to feel comfortable with this from the outset.

Secondly, do you have a separate space just for work (i.e. a garden room, cabin, separate office space) or are you intending to use your living room/dining room? If you are using a more personal space then it is a good idea to de- personalise it. Taking down family pictures, removing toys, etc. Remember this will be your work space so it needs to look like one not just your front room. Does your room have disabled access? If it doesn't then this may impact the range of clients you can offer therapy, so this is something further to consider.

Parking, access and lone working are all equally relevant to working from home. If you are working from home you may be lone working more so think carefully about how you feel about this. Some people install cameras in their hallway for safety reasons, or only see clients when someone else is in the house. Having a panic button or an alarm under your chair can help you feel more secure and know you either have a deterrent or a way of communicating your distress to others. Go with your gut instinct if something doesn't feel right - it's better to be safe than sorry.

Privacy and confidentiality must be kept to in the same way as they would be in a clinic environment.

Children and animals at home

If you have children, 'Will you see clients when they are there?' 'Will they be noisy?' Or furthermore 'Will you or your client be distracted if you hear them?' These are all things that need to be thought about before you make a decision.

If you have animals (I do!) you need to think about where they can be during a visit. You must check that your clients are not allergic or phobic as this could cause someone to feel very uncomfortable or unwell. When having initial phone or email contact you can address this. Remember even if your pet is not in the room there will be pet hair floating around.

Using your time well

Some therapists like working from home because they can pop some washing on in between clients or do some other chores. This is completely a personal choice, but I chose not to work from home as I wanted my work days to be focused on work and not home stuff. I am great at procrastinating so would get very easily distracted. For me I like to keep my work and home space separate so working elsewhere always made sense to me. Our job is overwhelming at times with the amount of other people's emotional weight we can carry and I wanted and needed physical separation of this. Again everyone is different so do what is right for you.

Insurance differences

When working from home your insurance needs to cover this. It would be a good move to call your home insurance company and discuss what they can offer you. Most providers offer business cover and as a therapist you can declare how many clients you would be seeing a week from your premises and they will offer you a price in accordance with this. If for example you are seeing fifteen clients a week they would then charge you X amount to cover you. You may want to start with a lower tariff and then as your business grows move to a higher covering rate.

The positives of home working

Of course there are many advantages to working from home. You won't have to pay any room rent or any travel costs. This will mean you are making more money per hour than if you were renting a room. Your bills at home may increase slightly and you have the added expense of business insurance however working from home does considerably cut your costs.

I know a lot of therapists that choose this option because they struggle with their own health. Being at home and having easy access to things can be helpful for some. It also means you can set up your space how you want which is a great bonus. Although most of the rooms I rent are quite flexible with how I set up the space, this is not always the case.

Doing home visits

I offer home visits for people who suffer with ill health or with agoraphobia.

Home visits can be really helpful for some clients and mean you are not excluding a really important client base. Firstly, if you are travelling to clients you may want to charge extra to cover your travel time and fuel costs. Secondly, you will need to take extra care to maintain your safety.

It is ideal if you can still do a telephone assessment or your usual assessment in clinic for your first meeting before you go to their home.

Just beware that people often behave differently when in their own environment. However it can be positive from a therapeutic point of view as it can reveal very useful information about the client and the way they behave and interact. Just remember practically it can be tricky.

I had an incident where I was forty five minutes into the session and the person's partner walked in followed by a child. They then continued to join in, asking what we were talking about. I had already set the boundaries but they were clearly pushing to see if I would hold to them. Afterwards I had to have a conversation with my client about what therapy was and how people coming in was inappropriate and detrimental to our work. The client then decided that it may be better if I saw her in clinic, which turned out to the the better option for our work.

Online and telephone therapy

The last aspect I want to cover is online and telephone therapy. This is a great way to reach clients outside your area not to mention limiting your outgoing costs. This is not my preferred way of working but I do offer it as an alternative to face to face counselling. My first online client came about from me seeing him in person first and then continuing our sessions via vsee (a securer version of Skype) when he went to university. It worked really well and encouraged me to continue to offer online therapy.

Personally, I have never offered pure telephone counselling because I feel it would be like working in the dark. I don't need to explain you how important it is in our work to 'see' our clients, their facial expressions and body language and this is why I made the decision not to pursue it. However, if you are confident in this area and feel able to offer telephone counselling then by all means use this skill to your advantage. With both options in mind these are the aspects that need to be discussed and put in place.

1. Ensure you and your client have brilliant internet connection and if your connection goes down you have a plan of action, such as recalling the client if this happens or using a landline phone and reverting to pure telephone counselling if it is not possible to reconnect.

2. You both have access to programs such as vsee or Facetime.

3. You are both aware that like any online service it is never 100% secure but to the best of your knowledge you will protect your conversations by ensuring that you remain within an unrecorded environment. To read more about this go to- www.vsee.com

4. It is advisable that you call the client, so ensure you have their username/number/email address.

5. You are in a quiet, confidential space where you won't be disturbed and likewise for your client.

6. Remember to discuss the issues around different time zones if applicable.

7. You cover your business and therapeutic contracts in the same way you would in a face to face session.

Finally, if you are not confident in this way of working be sure to talk it through with your supervisor and get further training.

Part Two

Creating a warm and inviting space

This is part two of choosing your location. Having had therapy yourself you will have experienced different therapy rooms. A good place to start is by asking yourself 'What did I like about it?' 'Was I comfortable?' 'If it was my room what would I have done differently?' Everyone has different taste and styles. I would encourage you to utilize this but also recognise that it needs to be universal. For example when I did my room I was aware that it was starting to become quite feminine (I am a girly girl - no apologies!) so I had to adjust elements so I wasn't just catering to one gender or taste. Having a neutral room is key however that doesn't mean boring! I have soft lighting, creative art, soft cushions, blankets, candles, books and fun knick- knacks placed around to give it a professional but homely feel.

Creating an inviting environment

I decided when I started in private practice that I wanted my clients to feel like they were accessing an hour of rest and luxury. As people are paying a good amount of money for my services I wanted them to come away feeling that their money was worth spending with me. Now obviously as a therapist the work we do is the most important aspect of counselling, but being able to feel pampered and relaxed I believe models to the client how to practice self care. It also sends the message to them that you care about them and their needs.

When I need some me time I often put on some cosy clothes, grab a blanket and curl up on the sofa. If you can give your clients this sort of freedom in your room then it will only serve them well. I have a client who comes in and immediately takes her shoes off and cuddles up on the sofa with a cushion. It's a real joy for me to see how comfortable she is to be able to do that. What I am trying to articulate is don't underestimate the power of your environment and how it can affect you and your clients.

Enjoy the process

Rather that thinking about setting up or designing your room as a chore, give yourself permission to enjoy the process. If you are not confident in this area of creative design then don't be afraid to ask for help. I'm not suggesting an interior designer (although if you have the money then go for it!) but maybe you have a friend whose house always looks and feels lovely or someone who always dresses well. Book in a shopping trip with them and get discussing some ideas.

Pinterest is a great place to get some ideas of spaces you love. I adore the colour blue so I came up with a couple of shades I wanted to incorporate into my scheme. Have a look for some picture hangings that inspire or spark joy in you. Often I see generic landscape pictures in people's rooms which are absolutely fine, just be careful not to conform to what you think 'should' be in a counselling room rather than what you are drawn too. For example I have a abstract watercolor of a lion on my wall and clients often comment on how much they like to look at it.

A clutter free space

When speaking to clients one of the main things they appreciated about my space was that not only was it calm but it was clutter free. I don't know about you but when I am either trying to work or relax if there is 'stuff' everywhere I struggle to concentrate. Keeping your room tidy will not only help your clients but it makes for a much nicer environment for you.

Plants and candles

As with any indoor space plants bring a touch of the outdoors in, not to mention the fact that they are good for oxygen levels! They can bring a splash of life to your room and there are many options. Now I am not very green-fingered so I have plants that I cannot kill easily! Hardy plants are a good option so you don't have to think about them too much other than watering every once in a while. I love candles but I realise this is a personal preference. Like softer lighting they create a warmer atmosphere. Scented candles can be nice as they awake the senses. Just be careful if working with clients who have experienced trauma as smells can act as a trigger. I also have a client with Asperger's syndrome and he is hypersensitive so I leave the candles unlit when he comes. Sometimes you may have to adjust your environment dependant on your client's needs, remember we are all different so be person- centred in this area.

Chairs and sofas

Having comfortable chairs or sofas is an obvious must, and if you have your own room, will be your biggest expense. It may sound simple but thinking about ergonomics is key. Poang chairs from Ikea are often popular as they are nice and cheap; however the bucket like chairs are actually not good for your hips because your knees are higher causing your hips to be closed, which can cause longer term issues in some. Also having a chair that doesn't have a supported back again is not going to help your spine and posture in the long term. Take some time to try and choose your chairs.

As therapists we sit for long amounts of time so it is worth investing some time considering this subject. If you don't have the funds then it may be advisable to choose some cheaper ones and invest in some more suitable options later when you can. When you are looking for a room to rent it is a good idea to see what chairs they can offer you so again you can try them and see if they are suitable

If you have limited decor options

Depending on your room setup and room agreement you may have limited options for what you can do in terms of decor, however there are some things you can do to add a bit of luxury and comfort.

Consider asking if you can use candles. If naked flames are not allowed, that's ok you can now buy battery operated ones. It can be nice to have some soft cushions and blankets. I have some velvet cushions in my room and I notice my clients stroking them during the session as a way of soothing themselves. If you work creatively it can be good to have some stones, small objects, pens and paper around.

Think about your lighting, is there an option to have lower lighting or side lamps as a way of creating a warmer atmosphere. Remember it's the small touches that can have a big impact. I know lugging all of these items around may not be very feasible, so ask if there is a place where you can store a few of your things on site. For me this then made setting up and down my room much easier and less time- consuming.

If you're anything like me then you will want to get started as soon as possible (I have a strong hurry up driver), but rushing such an important part of your business is not advisable. Just remember, take your time finding and decorating a room and the end result will be worth it.

Anna's Answers

- Do your research when looking for a room and consider all of the above before making a final decision.
- Think about location, costs, room agreements, travel, accessibility, lone working, home working and decor.
- Don't be afraid to ask for help when designing your therapy room - you want to make it the best it can be.
- Finally, enjoy the process and remember that nothing is set in stone. Sometimes rooms are short term and it's ok to outgrow somewhere.

Practical checklist

- ❏ Choose my location
- ❏ Call round and visit potential spaces
- ❏ Complete risk assessment
- ❏ Complete a room agreement and check premises insurance for renting out rooms
- ❏ Photocopy my insurance certificate and give the building owner a copy
- ❏ If working from home call my home insurance company

I thought it would be helpful to provide a shopping list of everything you may need for your room. If you are renting then some of these aspects won't apply to you so just use it how you would like.

Shopping list for my therapy room

❏ Chairs/sofa

❏ Side table

❏ Book shelves

❏ Lockable storage

❏ Lockable box or backpack for transporting client data

❏ Pictures and wall hangings

❏ Blankets

❏ Cushions

❏ Rug

❏ lamps

❏ Plants/flowers

❏ Candles

❏ Coasters

❏ Waste paper bin

❏ Knick-knacks

❏ Clock

❏ Do not disturb sign

❏ Tissues

❏ Creative materials

❏ Paper and pens

❏ Flipchart/whiteboard

❏ Clipboard

❏ Batteries

- ❏ Matches
- ❏ Water glasses and jug
- ❏ Business cards
- ❏ Copies of membership, insurance and qualifications
- ❏ Leaflets and information about other services
- ❏ Cleaning products
- ❏ First aid box or access to one
- ❏ Accident book

Notes:

....

....

....

....

....

....

....

....

....

....

....

....

....

....

....

....

....

....

....

....

....

....

....

Branding and marketing

For me branding and marketing is the area where I have grown the most while building my practice. When I started out I knew absolutely nothing about how to go about branding my business and getting myself out there. There were so many ways and means I felt rather overwhelmed by the whole process. I am going to break this down so that you can go through this process methodically and hopefully avoid some of my pitfalls!

Part One

Branding your company

So let's start with branding. A business term which means 'To create a unique name and image for a service or product, mainly through advertising with consistent themes.' (www.businessdictionary.com)

Now you have a company name start to think about what images or colours seem to fit with it. For example for me being Honeysett Counselling my designer put a bee in my logo and stuck with calm colours of grey, white and pale orange. Mine was quite literal but that doesn't have to be the case. Pinterest is a good place to see what logos are out there and will give you inspiration for your own.

You can build a logo yourself but unless you have expertise in this area, I would advise against this as it needs to look professional, so outsourcing is best. Find yourself a great graphic designer and ask them to come up with a few different ideas to show you. This will then help you to know what you like and what you don't. Remember like your name this will accompany you wherever you go and will be printed on business cards, website, social media, leaflets, letterheads, assessment paperwork and contracts, so make sure you are 100% happy with the design and colours.

Once you have decided on your finished product I would suggest you ask your designer to send you your logo in as many forms as possible for example large, small, with background, without background and in a JPEG and PNG format. (these are photo type abbreviations and whenever you print or use an image these are the two formats that are often required). This is a real opportunity to have some fun and be creative. Logos are supposed to be vibrant and eye- catching so don't limit yourself.

Consistent themes

When branding one of the key components is using consistent themes of colour, font and images. What often makes something look unprofessional is a hotchpotch of ideas mashed together with no consistency.

Imagine renovating your bathroom for example. Your bath suite would all be from the same store and so matching in style and color. You would pick a paint scheme for your walls and then tiles to tie in. Finally you would dress the room with towels, shelves, blinds mirrors etc to match with the other items.

Now you don't want everything exactly the same shade or that may look bland, but if you mix colours from the same pallet and mix mediums of texture overall you will have a room that comes to life! Branding your company is no different to this. You need to:

- Pick a colour palette that you like and that suits the profession. (personally I would avoid large amounts of one very bold colour and instead use a bold colour only for striking accents.)
- Pick a font style and stick with it or similar styles.
- Think of what sort of images you would like to use for your website, and any other marketing you may do.
- Remember any pictures of yourself need to be clear and professional. I recommend avoiding selfies (not professional looking) but don't be afraid to smile and be you. Clients have often said they have contacted me because my photo looks professional but friendly.

Logos and business cards

Before you go to your designer for your logo, be prepared. I say this because the clearer the brief the better the outcome will be.

Once you have a logo you can then take the plunge and design and print off your business cards. Your designer can help you with this or alternatively you can print them yourself. There are loads of easy to use companies out there such as Vistaprint and they also let you save your design so that when you need more, you can just request them.

Being dyslexic my spelling is terrible so I had my friend proofread all of my marketing material to make sure all of my information was correct and accessible. I suggest you do likewise or you will have a well meaning person pointing it out AFTER you have gone to print! You will need your phone number, an email and your website address (which we are about to cover.)

I was so excited when my business cards came through the post and couldn't wait to hand them out to everyone. Make sure you carry a few on you so that when the opportunity arises you will be ready to give them away.

Websites

Over the last couple of years I've had therapists ask me the question 'Do I really need a website?' My answer to that is always the same, a resounding YES! If you are going in to or already are in private practice then I would say having a website is one of the most effective ways of bringing in new clients and showing off your business. There are a number of reasons why I believe having a brilliant website is so crucial;

1. In today's age the internet is a modern day yellow pages. When people want to find a service provider the first thing they will do is use a search engine.
2. An online presence means you are accessible not just in your local area. For example, as a trainer I get work all

over Kent because the internet gives me the opportunity to reach a much wider audience.

3. Having a well designed website gives customers an insight into who you are as a person and what sort of service you provide.

4. Having a website gives clients more information about your service and customers may well choose you over someone who hasn't got a website because they feel more reassured.

5. Counselling directories are great (particularly while your website is climbing up the rankings); however they present the competition right next to you - once people are on your website they are thinking about you and only you.

Only last week I had an assessment with a client and they explained they chose me because of my professional looking website. If done well your website WILL bring you clients. My two main sources of referrals are from my website and a counselling directory (I will cover more later in this chapter.)

Domain name

Firstly what is a domain name? In simple terms it is your website address. For example, Google's domain name would be www.google.co.uk.This means Google has bought the rights to this address so that no one else can use it over the next year. At the end of that year it has to be renewed by paying a small fee.

50

When purchasing your domain name you need to be aware that there are other options for people to have something similar. When I bought www.honeysettcounselling.co.uk there was also an option of **www.honeysettcounselling.com**, **www.honeysettcounselling.org** and a few more variations. As my surname is pretty rare I haven't worried about someone else calling their therapy business by my name (although if I expand I may buy the rights to others.) However it is worth paying attention to your domain name as it may be popular. This will then make it more difficult to be found online because the search engines will not only find your company but also any others that are alike.

Something I have noticed is that as therapists we seem to have a love affair with trees, stones and water - I don't know what that's about! I found three counsellors with the name Treeview counselling, all within a similar location and with similar logos, so bear in mind you are trying to stand out from the rest of the pack and having a similar name could certainly hinder this.

The other aspect to consider is that having what you 'do' in your domain name is going to make it easier to be found online. For example, when you are looking for say a plumber and you type into a search engine *'plumbers near me'* The search engine will file through its index of addresses and content to what it can find. If the plumber's domain name was www.miketheplumber.com the search engine would see the word plumber in his web address and bring him up as a helpful source to the searcher. If his web address was www.miketheman.com

unless he had brilliant content on his website he would be making it much harder for the internet to pick him up.

I chose www.honeysettcounselling.co.uk because it immediately says what it is on the tin. if you can put your name *and* location in your domain name this is even better.

Where do I buy a domain name from

This is the easy part. There are many domain name providers and the easiest option is to use a search engine to find one. The big companies like Godaddy, 123-reg and Wix are all excellent choices. Type in your ideal name and see what availability there is. If you have someone else designing your website this is something they can do for you if you find it all a bit daunting.

Building your website

Before I delved into the world of websites I spent time looking at other therapists and what they had put online. I'm afraid I was rather shocked and a little disappointed by what I found. Firstly, there was a large number of therapists that didn't even have a website, meaning they were missing out on a multitude of clients.

Secondly, the majority of websites I saw were dated, with a hotchpotch of colours, pictures and badly edited wording. The problem with this is it sends out a message of unprofessionalism and lack of concern, even though you care deeply about your private practice and clients.

If you were searching for a professional online you would make judgements based on how they presented themselves. This is no different. How are you presenting your business and what do you want people to see?

Please don't mishear me on this, I am not asking you to be something you are not, but rather to be the best you can be in this area.

Website designers VS building your own

This is a frequently asked question so I felt it was important to give this subject some air time. In the last few years website building programmes have become hugely popular as they are less costly and you can also be fully in control of building your own website. My website has been built using a website builder and I love having the flexibility of changing pictures, content and managing my blogs and events. However, I think the success of using website builders depends on how talented you are at using such programmes.

When I started my website it was my biggest investment because I knew that if I did it right it would bring me consistent referrals. I now receive 90% of my referrals through my website and pay very little for other advertising. I paid a Wix expert to create mine who then taught me how to use it properly. It took me a while to gain confidence but once I figured it out it was manageable. I believe that this is where many therapists have gone wrong with websites - they have used a website builder and not designed it very well. As your website is so important I would suggest that this is where you spend some of your money. Have a look around and see who is about that could help you with this service.

Another option is to pay someone to make your website completely from scratch using coding. This will also give you a professional look, just remember it may be a bit more tricky when wanting to change content as you would need to rely on them to do this for you, also incurring an extra charge each time.

If you are determined to build it yourself that is admirable, just get some feedback from some honest people during the process. (preferably in the marketing or business world **not** just other therapists) They can then let you know what impression you are giving out about your business and what changes you could make.

Content content content

This is so important for many different reasons. The content on your website will make or break your website's success. My main advice is to avoid a large amount of text that people have to scroll through as they will not absorb all the information, disengage and probably leave your site. When thinking about your content imagine you are a client looking for a service yourself. 'What information do you need?' 'Who is the therapist and what are they offering?' 'What are talking therapies and their aim, costs,

HOW TO SET UP A SUCCESSFUL COUNSELLING PRACTICE

location and contact details?' These are just the essentials but a good place to start.

My website is made up of a number of pages, each with a clear title on each page. I have a small paragraph of text on each page but also pictures and videos for people to engage with. This not only helps the user find what they are looking for quickly but it also optimises search engine results. Steer clear of counsellor jargon. Most clients when they are looking for a therapist won't have any idea about modalities and the foundations of our work. Sure, it is helpful for them to have a basic understanding of your model and what you offer but they don't need a bombardment of Carl Rogers or Eric Berns theories. Keep it simple and easy to access.

Reviews and people's testimonies

I have a section on my website that displays what clients have said about Honeysett Counselling. I do this because it gives potential clients the opportunity to see that others have found your services helpful. Client testimonials are not only inspiring but powerful and encourage others to seek the help they need. Very rarely have I asked a client directly for a review or testimony because they may not feel able to say no and I don't want to put someone in that position.

What I have found is some clients at the end of therapy have asked me if I would like a recommendation or their testimony which I have gratefully taken them up on. The other comments I have received were after I ran an emotional eating course and the feedback forms were all anonymous. You can also use any reviews that people have left on your google business page.

SEO and keywords

I won't spend too long on this subject because if you are getting support with building your website you may not need to know much about SEO and keywords. However it is good information to have so here are the basics.

SEO stands for 'search engine optimization.' When you build a website every page, picture, title and content will need to be made accessible for the internet. In its simplest terms each aspect of your website will need to be tagged with keywords that will make it stand out. As mentioned previously the internet is like an octopus with hundreds and thousands of tentacles. When someone types something into the browser this octopus will go through all of the information it can find online and pick the best matches for what has been searched. Having good SEO means that you are sending out relevant and current information about your business.

Keywords are words that are related to what you are trying to advertise. So as a counsellor in Kent I make sure I use the words counsellor, therapist and Kent throughout my website content. Another way of using keywords well is to put a sentence at the bottom of each page with all the keywords you can think of and then hide it (make the text invisible) The search engine will then pick up on your pages quicker because of this juicy content.

It is simple to do. If you are using a website builder there will be a button that says 'manage SEO and keywords.' If someone else is building your website it is a good idea to ask them to show you where they are and how you update them.

Mobile view for your website

People often forget about this, however with the a huge amount of people using their mobiles to search nowadays addressing your mobile view is crucial. Most website builders will have a separate service where you can change your website to fit a mobile well. Remember a brilliant website can look terrible on a mobile as the pictures, text and buttons can all move around with you ending up with a mashed up unclear site. If using a web designer make sure you discuss this with them and let them know you want your website to be mobile ready.

Finally keep your website alive! It is a living, breathing entity and you need to let the search engines know you are still current. You can maintain this by blogging, vlogging (thats video diaries for those of you that are thinking what?), uploading pictures from time to time, checking your performance, getting friends to come onto your page and click around and upkeeping your SEO's.

Part Two - Marketing strategies

Leaflet and business card drops

When I started marketing my business I made a list of all the GP surgeries, community centres, and public spaces in Ashford and I spent a morning driving around asking if I could display my leaflets and cards. I can honestly say this has been the least successful way of gaining business and I have only had one or two enquiries via this route. However in the beginning that is still better than nothing and it also starts to get your name out into your area. Just don't expect this to be the only way to gain business. You should also limit the amount of money you spend as large amounts of paper advertising will cost and will not bring in much revenue in return.

The sort of places you can drop your business cards and leaflets are GP surgeries, (although some GP surgeries may already have counsellors they refer to) funeral parlours, solicitors, community centres, children's centres, coffee shops, police stations, dentists, healthcare businesses and libraries. I found this process daunting at the start but after two or three stops it became a breeze, plus most people were really friendly and helpful.

Newspapers and magazines

This brings me to another form of advertising that you need to approach with caution - local newspapers and magazines.

Not long after I had started private practice I received a phone call from a man asking if I wanted to advertise my business in a emergency services magazine. He made it sound very appealing, plus he knew how to stroke my newbie ego! (blush) I sent my advert and paid £195 for three months. Although this wasn't a scam as I received the monthly magazine and saw my advertisement, I was so disappointed having spent a good amount of money and time on it, not to receive a single enquiry.

The same happened with my local newspaper and again.... no calls. I am sure that others may have found it successful but in my experience it is a very expensive way of advertising which is now competing with the likes of Google. My advice would be to save your money and continue plugging your website and other social media pages.

Social media

I don't have to explain to you how big social media is now for communicating and advertising and so this is an important area of developing your business.

When people share and post things it is basically free advertising! I don't use social media pages to gain clients (although this is starting to happen now) but to give people a snapshot of who I am, what I offer and add to my online footprint. Pay particular attention to your social media cover photos as this will be the first thing people see. Having a brief statement about you and what you offer can be really helpful as well as your contact information.

All my social media pages have links to my website to encourage people to visit, often I will get three or four views on my page first and then I will receive an enquiry.

Whatever social media you take on it is always advisable to have business accounts where you can. This is because you have access to buy ads if necessary and you can see helpful stats that will tell you how many people visit and engage with your page.

I have a business page with Facebook, Instagram and a YouTube channel. I post my blogs, vlogs, pictures of what I'm up to at work and events that I may attend. I try and post something once a week on Facebook and most days on Instagram. What you post doesn't have to be mind blowing - it just reminds people that you are there and keeps your online presence active.

When it comes to Instagram try to mix up your content, therapists tend to post a lot of inspirational quotes which is great but there will be only so many of these your following will want to engage with. Post videos, great pictures and keep it fun and motivational. Think about the instagram accounts you enjoy engaging with and do likewise where you can.

Learning to use hashtags (#) can be a helpful way of growing your business. Don't be scared; a hashtag is just a modern search term. For example if someone was looking for a counsellor in Ashford they could use the term #counsellorsinashfordkent and it would bring up exactly that.

When you hashtag a word or a sentence you don't use spaces in between words. If you are posting on your Instagram you can use up to thirty different hashtags- this is so others can find you and begin following your content. If you are still scratching your head then don't worry, there is plenty of information online that will explain exactly how to use them to your advantage.

Blogging and vlogging

I like writing about things I am passionate about, blogging is such a simple way of getting your practice out there and attracting potential clients. Most website builders have a blog option on them and are easy to use. I post my blogs in various places such as my website, counselling directories, Facebook, Linkedin and Twitter. I have also recently started doing mini videos on various counselling subjects such as anxiety and depression. I then upload them to YouTube which also provides a link to your business.

Therapist directories

I am a big advocate of therapists directories. Not only are they great for online advertising but they also provide a quick link to your website and other media. Writing a directory profile requires the same care and attention as the content on your website. A good directory profile has a professional picture and clear and friendly content explaining what you offer (with good keywords). Use the opportunity to show off your expertise as some people use the advanced search to find therapists for a specific issue.

Most directories offer prompts when writing your profile and some also have articles on how to get the best results from your page, so read them! I also post pictures of my locations and short videos from time to time. Furthermore, I have found posting a blog on your page is really profitable because often the directories post these on other social media outlets (extra free advertising).

The down side is they do cost from around fifteen to twenty pounds per month. However even if you only get one client a month, it will still be well worth the investment.

Registering with Google My Business

A effective and free way to be found online is to register with Google my business. All you need to do is register by adding details such as your company name, address, phone number and opening times and with in a couple of days you will be listed with a visible map of your practice location.

Letter writing to organisations

I haven't found writing letters to organisations the most profitable way of gaining referrals however it can bring one or two people your way. The positive is you are getting your name known with different organisations and although they may not use your services they may pass your information on to others.

EAP work

EAP stands for Employment Assistant Professionals. Their job is to provide qualified practitioners to companies who support employees.

There is a lot of work out there for therapists however like everything there are pros and cons. Firstly a lot of companies ask for only accredited counsellors, this is changing though and there is still work from this resource for non accredited therapists, you may just have to look a little harder. Secondly, the work is very likely to be short term because the companies will only pay for a set number of sessions or pay up to a certain value. This does not need to be an issue but if you are used to long term work then just be aware of the limitations short term work can bring. Thirdly, you may not always get paid swiftly and it can take up to two months for you to be reimbursed. Again this will depend on the company and their system, but it can be incredibly frustrating having to chase people for money you have already earnt.

On the plus side, it can bring you in some regular work and alleviate some of the pressures of private practice. Once you are accredited (if you choose to go down that route) you are likely to be contacted by EAP companies asking if you would like some work and let's face it it's always nice to be headhunted! Don't forget to add their logos to your website and even update your

SEO's adding the company name, so that you have another means of being found via search engines.

Networking

I was always a bit scared of the concept of networking. The idea that I would meet up with complete strangers to exchange business ideas and make contacts for my benefit felt unnerving and rather egotistical. I can see now I was missing the point.

Networking has lots of dimensions and does not always involve making yourself super vulnerable with loads of strangers. I have found it to be much more about building relationships with others, which 'hooray' I'm really good at (and if you are a therapist you are too). Most of my networking has been through others I already know who have had qualities and skills I like and could benefit my business and vice versa. I've then said 'hey do you fancy getting a coffee sometime to talk business?' Most people are looking for opportunities too so will likely bite your hand off and then away you go!

All of my counselling rooms have come about by me being bold enough to ask someone for a coffee. However if you're unsure about networking CPD events are great opportunities to meet others in a non - threatening way so maybe start there where there is a common interest.

Payment plans and discounts

I have never gone down the route of discounts and payment plans purely because I haven't needed to. My honest opinion is I'm not sure if this will bring you custom but what I do know is people love a discount and if you want to try this method then I can't see any therapeutic reason not to. You could try something like buy five sessions and get the sixth half price. Just be careful not to undersell yourself here. I would advise not to make it a continual offer but more of a 'special' every once in a while. I say this because otherwise people might start to expect a discount from your services all the time which may not always be possible.

Word of mouth

This is the last category for marketing I promise (it turned into a much bigger chapter than I anticipated). This is the holy grail of the therapy world and when you start to get regular word of mouth referrals you will know that all your advertising and efforts have paid off. Clients only ever refer if they have received a good service so when you receive a word of mouth referral it is brilliant confirmation that you are doing a good job! (hopefully you know this already but we all need some encouragement from time to time.)

It took me about a year to have any and when I did it was a lovely feeling. Now this doesn't mean that once you reach this stage you can sit back and wait for the phone to ring or become complacent about your practice as a therapist, but it does mean you are beginning to get established. Two cautions to bear in mind -

1. Therapists often don't get as many word of mouth referrals as other professions because a lot of clients don't disclose that they are in or have been in therapy. However this is starting to change though as the stigma wears off.

2. You may get referrals that are too closely linked such as good friends and family members which puts you in a compromising position. Always make sure you are not compromising your ethics just because you **need** another client. This is a great time to refer to others in your area and take advantage of your networking.

Phew! And we are done. Here are Anna's answers for a quick reminder and break down of this chapter.

Anna's Answers

- Brand your business using consistent themes, colour palettes and fonts.

- Build an awesome website - don't be cheap with this aspect, if you do a great job, it will be well worth the investment.

- Make sure you understand SEO, keywords and how to direct internet traffic.

- Design and print business cards and leaflets and hand them out to appropriate places, but don't go mad as this is the least cost effective way to advertise.

- Be careful not to be sweet talked into magazine advertisement - it is expensive and in my experience generates very little return.

- Social media is your friend! Use it to widen your internet footprint and have fun with it!

- Take advantage of EAP work it can alleviate the pressures of sourcing clients.

- Networking is much like building relationships so embrace it where you can.

- Finally word of mouth is a fabulous encouragement that the work you are doing is successful!

Practical checklist

- ❏ Pick my branding colours
- ❏ Find a graphic designer for my logo

❑ Write my website content

❑ Find a website designer or create it myself

❑ Design a mobile view for my website

❑ Learn how to use my website

❑ Design my business cards and print

❑ Drop my business cards to local companies and organisations

❑ Join a counselling directory and write my profile

❑ Set up my social media accounts

❑ Contact EAP companies

❑ Network with other therapists

❑ Try writing and publishing a blog

❑ Try recording and uploading a video

Notes:

....

....

....

....

....

....

....

....

....

....

....

....

....

....

....

....

....

....

....

....

....

....

....

....

....

....

....

Administration and documents

Right, I am going to try and make this section as interesting as possible because I know that the thought of reading about paperwork sounds pretty boring! However like some of the other chapters these are aspects that need attention.

Administration

As a dyslexic, I am not the most organised person and I have to work hard to feel on top of things, particularly administration. When I worked in an office environment it was the running joke that 'Anna's left something on my desk again!' I would often get distracted and wander off to do something else that took my attention.

I knew that entering private practice would require me to have certain systems and protocols in place so that I didn't get in a muddle. In this chapter I will share with you the administrative tasks that you will come across and how I have chosen to manage them. Obviously these are just my suggestions and so you must do it the way you find most beneficial however; I will lay out my trail and hopefully it will help with your process.

Finances

When I started building my practice I was still working part time elsewhere and so I needed to ask myself the question:

'In order to be in private practice full - time how many clients do I need to survive?'

Depending on your financial position you may need to ask this question too.

Although this can be frustrating and a little 'must get bums on seats!' it did really give me a good kick to get out there and start promoting my business. You may be in a different position and if you don't have the same urgency to make money you can build your business at a much slower pace. Whatever financial position, you need to start with the basics:

1. Do your calculations so you know where you stand at the beginning.
2. Be organised and specific in your record keeping.

Record keeping

The simplest way to do this is to keep a monthly spreadsheet making sure you enter all your incomings and outgoings. There are loads of templates out there or you can create your own using programmes like Excel. Now this is not my strong point so I enlisted my mother to help me set this up and learn how to use it properly. Again if you need help in this area like me, don't be afraid to ask. I enter my data at the end of each week using my diary to relay how many people I've seen and other expenditures. It is a mundane task, however it does become easier as you progress.

Keeping receipts

My motto here is keep everything! Keep a paper receipt for everything you buy or pay out for your business. I have a plastic pocket that is kept in a folder with the month written on it. Then you can just bung them all in together and record it on your spreadsheet.

Tax

I know- 'Groan.' The most common questions relating to tax seem to be 'How do I save for tax?' and 'What can I claim back?'

The way I have saved for tax as mentioned in Chapter 2 is to have an additional savings account alongside my business account. Then each week depending on what I have earnt I transfer 25% of the money into the savings account (this is also to cover national insurance).

When you start earning remember that you only have to start paying tax when you earn over £11,500 per year (correct to 2018/19). In my first few months of working I didn't get anywhere near this, however once I became entirely self employed I started putting tax away regularly. This creates good habits for when you will need to pay tax and it also ensures you have enough funds to cover your national insurance contributions.

For income in 2018/19 above this threshold, you will be taxed at the following levels;

- The Basic Income Tax rate of 20% on income up to £45,000

- The Higher Income Tax rate of 40% on income between £45,001 and £150,000
- The Additional Income Tax rate of 45% on income over £150,000.

Even if you have saved too much tax it is always a pleasant surprise to realise this at the end of the year, rather than having to scramble around to find money you don't have.

Tax returns

I know many therapist's who do their own tax returns; however I felt that it was not worth the stress and time so I chose to pay an accountant. The great thing about this is I then don't need to ask what can I claim back, as she does it all for me. I just keep everything I have spent on my business and give all the information to her. If there is then something I can't claim for or missed then she will advise me.

If you do wish to know more about what you can claim for the GOV.UK website is great and you can glean a lot of information from there. The general rule is you can claim back on anything that you **need** to run your business. So for us mental health professionals that includes supervision, CPD training, relevant books, room decor, stationery, etc.

Holidays and sick pay

I learnt the hard way with this because in my previous employment I had the privilege of both paid holiday and sick pay and so I hadn't had to think about it.

As a self employed person you don't get this luxury. In the beginning I really didn't have enough money to put aside for holiday and sick pay, but once you are earning enough you could start putting some money away. This will mean you won't feel trapped and think 'I can't afford to be sick' or 'I can't afford to have a holiday.'

Personally, I didn't want another bank account (three is enough) so I chose to do it the old school way and put some cash aside in a pot. However, I realize that this method is not for everyone. Regardless of how you save, it really does take the stress out of time off and is a definite must for me now.

Banking money

Just a brief note on this one. If you are taking cash payments from your clients I warn you now you will become a regular cash machine and will need to bank your money regularly. It can be quite a big adjustment being paid weekly as most of the general public get paid monthly. Just give yourself time to get into this rhythm and it will become your new norm before long.

I choose to bank my earnings at the end of my working week and then transfer money accordingly. I find the quickest way is to use the machines provided by the bank as it saves all the queuing. Alternatively you can use the slips provided and post your money though the bank's letter boxes however; your money won't be in your account immediately.

Client notes

Legally there is no requirement as a therapist to keep notes; however many do as it helps to have a record of what you and your client have been working on. Your membership body's ethical framework will have guidelines to help you with this on its website.

Personally, I keep weekly notes on each client and they are stored in a locked file on my computer. I write a brief sentence about what we have discussed and no more. The only time I record more is if there is a safeguarding issue.

General Data Protection Regulation (GDPR)

This is a new law, which came into force on 25th May 2018. The aim is to give people more control over their personal data - how it is given, shared, stored - and it provides individuals with rights over their data, such as the right of access, the right to be informed and the right to be forgotten. I cannot promise a detailed account of this law (I am certainly not a expert in this area) and it is your responsibility to research and put in place the correct guidelines. What I can share with you are some of the measures I have put in place in my own company.

Registering with the Information Commissioner's Office (ICO)

As therapists we are collecting, holding, and processing personal data so this means we need to be registered with the ICO. You can do this through the ICO's website at www.ico.org.uk and it will cost you £40 for the year (correct in 2018). If you do not comply with the data protection law you can be fined a hefty amount so it is important that you register and your practice is GDPR compliant.

Client notes/contracts

Your client notes whether electronic or paper need to be held securely. For example, this could mean keeping all paper copies in a locked cabinet where only you can access them. The same goes for any notes on your computer, make them unidentifiable and keep them password protected.

If like me from time to time you move personal data from one venue to another I would advise you investing in a small locked box to be kept in your car or a lockable backpack. This then will ensure that people's data is kept secure at all times.

Website/emails

Your website needs to have a privacy policy and use of cookies page where you explain what you do with people's information.

Some of the questions you need to address on your website are as follows:

- What will you do with the contact details people provide via the website? (phone or email)
- How long will you retain that information?
- How and why are you collecting personal data? (For example, to communicate with and market your business to those that have expressed an interest in finding out more.)
- How can people let you know if they do not wish for their information to be kept? (phone number/email)

See the helpful checklists on the ICO's website for more about the privacy information you need to provide when you collect personal data.

Your privacy page link needs to be clearly visible and most websites put this link next to their enquiry box making it easy for people to find. You must also keep up to date with emails you receive from clients and delete any that are no longer needed (don't forget to then empty your trash folder).

Data consent on your business contract

When I go through my business contract with clients I now have a tick box where they can consent to me processing their personal data. If people are reluctant to do so I explain carefully why I need to keep certain data and that I will hold it no longer than is necessary.

How long do I hold data

Your insurance company may stipulate how long you need to keep personal data for, for example for the purpose of any legal claim that could be brought against you. Contact your insurers and ask them how long they require you to keep client data. My insurance company ask that I keep it for five years. Once that time has lapsed you then need to safely destroy any data you have.

Transparency with clients

Ultimately, the main point of the GDPR is to be transparent about the data we collect and store, so that our clients feel as safe as possible. As therapists we very rarely share any information with others because the work we do is confidential. However it is still a person's legal right to know how we handle their information and their choice to opt out.

To find out more information about the GDPR please visit the Information Commissioner's Office at www.ico.org.uk

Updating social media

In between clients I often update my social media by posting something like a picture or an interesting article. I find the more personal the better the response. The main aim is to keep connecting with your audience and potential clients and remind the internet that you are still live.

Reading

A simple one really but it's good to be reading up to date information about your field. I also read anything that is related to psychology and then for continued professional development (CPD) purposes I'll do a small review on what I've learnt. It will depend on which membership body you are with as to their CPD requirements but the BACP encourage reading and a mini review can count towards your CPD.

Updating website

I spend time every now and then just updating my website such as changing some pictures or checking my SEO are performing well. I also update my counselling directory profile to keep things fresh.

Responding to enquiries

Most of the enquiries I receive are either via email or phone calls. I think it really depends on the client as to how contact is made. Some like to hear your voice and have a direct conversation with you, however for many email is preferable due to its convenience or safe distance.

Email responses

When I first started I spent a great amount of time writing back the 'perfect' email to each client explaining everything they had asked and anything I could think of that they may need to know.

I had enough time to do this when I started as I had fewer clients but I don't recommend it. As your practice grows you will find that you just don't have the time to do this. On reflection some of my long responses were about me wanting to people please and make sure 'they liked me.' (thank goodness for supervision).

I now have a short concise email that explains what an assessment session entails and then I ask if they would like to book in to see me. All of my pricing, locations etc are on my website so I redirect them there for most other questions. Once we have agreed a date for them to come to the assessment I then send out a confirmation email with all the details. This includes directions, parking, access to the building, payment methods, including my BACS details and also my cancellation policy.

It is handy doing it this way because then all I have to do is change the name, time and date at the top and the rest remains the same, which makes it relatively hassle free. It also gives you a paper trail and your client something concrete for their diaries rather than just a conversation. Remember to stay consistent with your branding and ensure your logo is at the top of all of your correspondence as well as your business details.

Phone Contact

If a potential client calls you instead of emailing you may not feel so prepared. I say this because I learnt the hard way with this one. When I first started I was so desperate to get clients that sometimes over the phone I sounded rushed and keen to get anyone booked in!

On one occasion, I was in a busy cafe with a friend and instead of letting it go to voicemail trusting they would leave a message I picked up the call. I felt flustered and I came off the phone feeling like I had waffled. I never heard from that person again and to be honest I wasn't surprised. I know you cannot have the perfect conversation, however there are a few tips I now try to abide by when making contact for the first time.

1. If you are busy or in a public place and you believe the call to be from a potential client then leave it. Not only is there a confidentiality issue with answering the call, it also sounds unprofessional.

2. Make sure your answer phone message is specifically recorded for your business. That way people will know they have rung the right number and they can leave a message if they wish to.

3. Once you are in a quiet confidential place with your diary then you can return the call. Personally, I do not ring back an unknown number because the client may not want this. Be patient and trust that if they are the right client then will contact you again.

4. For most people it takes a lot of courage to ring and ask for help, so bear this in mind when talking to someone for the first time. Like my email I do not spend a long time on the phone with someone. I ask how I can help and then if they

would like to book to see me for assessment and I explain this process. If a client starts to share large amounts over the phone I tend to explain that it would be best for us to explore this more in the assessment. This might sound cold, however I have learnt that you can give copious amounts of time on the phone to then never actually work with them. Obviously, I model care and kindness to each person I speak with and I like to think that I am always friendly and personable, however you need to have some boundaries to maintain a professional process.

I remember one incident where I kept having calls from a potential client who I just could not get off the phone. I was trying to be kind and empathic but this just seemed to encourage them more! Once I ended up on the phone for forty minutes. I never actually saw them for a session but if felt like I had accidently given her a session over the phone which was partly my fault because I had not been more assertive.

If you are struggling with this idea it may be helpful to think about when you call for another professional appointment, for example with a chiropractor or dietician, The likelihood is you will not spend a long time on the phone but will have time to mention what the issue is and ask the appropriate questions about an appointment. Therapy is the same. Just because our clients are calling about sensitive issues, doesn't mean we should get sucked into treading on eggshells. I know as therapists we don't always do well with business; however as I have mentioned several times throughout this book sometimes you need to wear that hat as well as your therapeutic one.

Nuisance calls and emails

As your information can be accessed easily it does open you up to nuisance calls or stalking, I am not saying this to alarm you and I have never personally experienced this issue, however it is a possibility. You are likely to have a gut instinct about whether someone is genuine about their enquiry, so I would always listen to your immediate response. Here are a couple of steps in how to deal with this.

1. If something or someone doesn't feel right to you listen to yourself and use your common sense.
2. If it is a nuisance call hang up immediately and do not try and engage with the person.
3. Call your local police station (not 999) and report the call/calls or emails.
4. Inform other counsellors in the area if you can.
5. Get some support from your supervisor as it can feel very intrusive and disconcerting.
6. If it continues in anyway talk to the police and consider changing your details (only in extreme cases is this likely to be necessary.)

Do I need a separate phone for my business

Lots of people ask this question and personally I don't have a separate phone. I am however starting to wonder if it would be better to have one because when the call is from an unknown number you don't know if it's a business or personal call. It also makes it harder to keep your work and personal life separate. If you have a separate mobile then when you are not working you can switch it off and put it down. The downside of having two would be double the phone bills and also having to carry two mobiles around when you're working. Again, this is a very personal choice and maybe when you are starting out an extra phone is just additional cost that can be incurred later down the line if needed.

Online booking systems

Some counsellors like to use online booking systems instead of a paper diary so your clients can book themselves in online and pay via PayPal. There are various systems out there some you have to pay for and others are free. I recommend 8 to 10 as it is simple and free. The other advantage of clients booking online is that they pay upfront so this may lessen your DNA's, but I do this via BACS anyway, which has the same result. The sticking point with this is that you will have little or no contact with clients before you meet them. I find a brief chat on the phone or an exchange of emails can be very informative and help you gain some sense of each other.

Regular or irregular slots

This decision will probably be based on your room limitations (if you're not working from home). My initial ideal was that each client would have a regular slot at the same time on the same day. On paper this seems ideal but in practice I have found that people's diaries change and consequently so will yours. Some clients like a more regular slot and I try to accommodate that where I can but I do not promise it to them. Say you have a really popular time slot (5.30pm seems to be mine) and the client you see at that time doesn't show or contact you for a few weeks, are you going to keep that slot open just for them and then lose money? Just worth thinking about your policy in this area.

First session

I do not need to tell you how important your first session is with a potential client and although we cannot control how other people will respond to us, we can manage the tone we set and put our clients at ease. When I first started in private practice I was quite nervous about meeting potential clients for the first time because I had a 'must get bums on seats' mentality. However, I quickly learnt that this is never a good mindset to have as it immediately puts you (and your clients) under pressure.

When I first meet a client I am warm and interested in them, I chat to them about their journey and say that I am pleased to meet them in person. As a person centred practitioner this comes naturally to me. I do offer my clients water and make sure they are comfortable in the room. I'm not saying overcompensate by not letting them feel nervous or apprehensive about the process; however we can be kind and human. If it helps maybe think back to the first time you entered therapy. Sometimes we get so used to therapy we can forget what it is like to make that first step in asking for help. I remember feeling really vulnerable and unsure about what to expect and I was relieved to have someone who was so kind and warm to me. (Thank you Shirley)

It is naive to think that the session does not start until you are in the room because the truth is that your client is already sizing you up and observing everything you do before you have even started the 'therapy.' I often start my sessions by asking how they feel about being here as a way of acknowledging their emotions and to again help put them at ease. I then go on to describe how the session will proceed so they have an outline of what to expect which again helps people to feel secure and relaxed.

Assessments

As therapists there are so many ways of assessing clients and I am aware that you will assess depending on your modality. I was not taught to assess clients but rather have a first session and let the client talk gleaning the information as you go. However, I have not found that to be the best way to gain a true representation of a client and what they may need. Some therapists offer a free consultation or a telephone assessment. This is totally fine if that is what you want to offer, but be careful not to rush the process and remember to value your time. I actually charge more for an assessment session as it is ten minutes longer than a counselling session to give us ample time to explore what we need to.

I recently heard of a counsellor who offered a free assessment but then found they had to pay for the room consequently making a loss. Not only does this undervalue your expertise and experience it also just doesn't make good business sense. Your time is your time regardless of whether it is a session or an assessment. People associate cost with quality so if you undercharge it could be interpreted by potential clients as a sign you are not very proficient or experienced.

What to cover in an assessment

Firstly, I take basic information such as name, DOB, date of assessment, referral route (important for your marketing information), GP details, medication, occupation, phone and email address.

I then have various titles to act as prompts so I cover all that needs to be covered. I quite often say to my clients that I do not stick to it like a script (not very humanistic) but I use the titles purely as reminders. I often move through them in different orders depending on what comes up. These are some of the titles I have on my assessment paperwork:

Presenting problem- This gives you a basic understanding of what the client has come into therapy for.

Drug and alcohol use- helpful to know if they use either of these as coping strategies.

Psychiatric history- This is to understand if there has been any mental health diagnosis in the past or in the family.

Previous counselling- It is really useful to know if a client has had previous therapy so you can understand how that experience was for them and how it feels to be in therapy. I like to find out if it was a positive or negative experience and then specifically why they felt this way. Some clients that have had negative experiences can understandably be more guarded and it is helpful to acknowledge this in the room. Equally, if a client has been with a therapist for many years and built a strong relationship with them, this can have a comparative impact on your new relationship.

It also avoids unethical practices in case the client is already in therapy.

Risk assessment- It is important to know if a client has ever attempted to take their own life or engaged in dangerous behaviour. I also ask if they feel they are at risk today.

Current social support systems- This is really good to know because starting the therapy process can be challenging and clients often need support outside the therapy room. I often draw a spider diagram with them in the middle and people around them.

Description of family of origin and description of immediate family - For both of these I ask questions such as what is your relationship with that person? or how would you describe your connection with your mother? This again gives you an indication of their relationships.

Goals in therapy- Often people have quite clear goals that they want to achieve. This is a good place in the assessment to ask them. I often ask how will we know when our work is complete? What differences would you like to see/feel?

Faith- As we are asking people about their emotional, mental and physical lives I feel it is vital to ask people about their spiritual well-being as well. For many their faith has a huge influence in their lives and often people's faith is part of their support system.

History- This is the largest section on my assessment paperwork and it is also the most fluid. I often ask clients about their upbringing, family life, school, relationships, jobs, important memories etc. I mainly let the client talk and tell me their story. This can be emotive so be sure to give time at the end of the assessment to ground them. I find that asking them a few questions about the here and now helps with this, by bringing them into the present.

Clients committing to therapy

Once you have completed your assessment session it is then time to ask if the client would like to continue with therapy (providing the work is within your competences). What I would say about this part is be confident, don't beat around the bush hoping they will say yes. You are a great therapist and they would be fortunate to have you - this is where a small amount of self belief goes a long way. I give my clients two options:

1. Would they like to commit to the process of therapy today and put a date in the diary for next week?

2. Or would they like to go away and have a think about it and then contact me at a later date?

In my experience most clients choose the first option. If they choose the second option I rarely hear from them again. If this happens try not to take it personally. You may not be a good fit, or the client simply may not be ready to commit to therapy and that's OK, it doesn't mean you have failed.

Once a client has agreed to sign up, I then go through the contact of care with them (your business contract). Your therapeutic contract can wait until your first session.

Measuring tools

Just a brief note on this. Often when working within an organisational setting you will be asked to measure your outcomes. In private practice you have no pressure on you to do this; however from time to time I do find it helpful depending on the client. If I have a client who is depressed or anxious I sometimes use a Core 34 at the beginning and end of therapy. Not only does it encourage you, it often encourages the client to see that they have moved forward in therapy. (The Core 34, and information on how to measure the scores, is available online).

Anna's Answers

- Spend time thinking about your contracts and what you need to put in them.
- Think about how you are going to assess your clients.
- Spend time investing in organised systems to keep administration as simple as possible.
- Be confident in your approach so your clients have confidence in you.

Practical checklist

- ❏ Design a monthly spreadsheet for my tax returns
- ❏ Design a system for receipt keeping
- ❏ Write my GDPR policy and take immediate steps to put in place
- ❏ Write and print my assessment paperwork
- ❏ Decide what booking system you would like to use either online or paper
- ❏ Create a CPD folder I can add too throughout the year
- ❏ Print measuring tools and file

Notes:

....

....

....

....

....

....

....

....

....

....

....

....

....

....

....

....

....

....

....

....

....

....

....

....

Chapter Six

Business and Therapeutic Contracts

I am hoping that this is a subject you will have covered in your training or previous work life as it is imperative for an ethical and successful relationship with your clients.

All businesses have contracts, some are verbal other are written and we are now going to look at what you need to consider when addressing contracts in your therapy business. There are two different types of contracts that are relevant to private practice and they are your **business contract** and your **therapeutic contract.**

Part One

Business Contracts

Let's start with a frequently asked question. Do I need to have a written business contact or just a verbal one?

Personally I would recommend a written contract. A written contract can act as a great prompt for all that needs covering in the initial assessment. Furthermore, it provides a paper trail. If a client pushes or breaks the contract then it is a great tool to bring them back to what you agreed together and remind them of the boundaries they agreed to.

I always get my clients to read it thoroughly and then sign and date the document. I also sign and date the copy too. I then keep it safely until we have completed therapy and then it gets put into my archive (more on note keeping later).

Now we have established **why** you need a written contract let us look at **what** goes in one.

Confidentiality and safeguarding

Let's start with one you will all know off by heart: confidentiality

This needs to be at the very top of your contract as it is the most important. You need to let your clients know the boundaries around confidentiality so that you are both clear from the beginning, that you will only break confidentiality if:

- They are at risk from harm.
- Someone else is at risk from harm.
- You are sharing your work with a supervisor and why you do this.

I also explain that supervision is a way of maintaining ethical practice and that all of their personal details shall remain anonymous. I have in my experience very rarely had to break confidentiality, but you may need to so you should be prepared. Working in an organisation there are certain protocols to follow but in private practice it can feel more of a burden when making a judgement call so I would advise you do a few things that will help.

1. Write down the facts immediately with time and date.
2. Talk to your supervisor first.
3. Always let the client know that you are going to have to break confidentiality. Furthermore tell them where you are

taking the issue so that they do not get a nasty surprise. Explain your reasons calmly and your duty of care.

4. After you have disclosed or reported what you need to, spend some time reflecting in supervision how it felt for you.

Remember it will feel pretty unnatural to you to break a client's confidentiality but you have a duty of care to your client or any other person that is at risk from harm and it is for their good. If you are still unsure about the area of safeguarding I would recommend attending a short course or signing up to online training to brush up on this subject.

First aid and accident books

As far as I am aware there is no law stating we need to be first aid trained as counsellors. (phew!) What is important is to keep an accident book in your room for any mishaps or injuries your client could sustain while with you. Hopefully your premises will also have one but it's always good to have one to cover you as a separate business just in case it comes back to bite you.

If you don't want to purchase an official accident book a simple notebook will surface where you write the date, time and nature of the incident that occurred, finally sign and print your name.

It is also advisable to have access to a first aid box whether it is yours or the premises you work from. When working with children enquire if they are allergic to anything or have medication on them such as an Epipen and ask the caregiver if an emergency happened what you would be required to do. Always to add such medical details to your assessment paperwork.

Social media boundaries

As time has moved on so has the way we connect with each other and so you need to take that into consideration when writing your business contract. Your clients might look you up on social media or even try to befriend or follow you. Explaining why this isn't appropriate is key so that these boundaries do not get blurred. If it is in your contract then it may avoid a difficult conversation afterwards where the client may end up feeling rejected.

Time keeping

In training you will have been taught the importance of time and how it is your responsibility as the therapist to be the timekeeper. In your contract set out how long you are seeing a client for. Often clients are surprised to know our time will be 50 minutes as they don't know about the counselling hour! (I always thought it was a strange one).

Again be clear about what you expect. You also need to think about what happens if a client is late. Do you still finish on time and charge the same? Do you run over time if you don't have anyone after them? Everyone deals with this differently.

I personally will start a session late and agree that we will do what we can with the time given. If it is possible then I may say we can continue on and do the fifty minutes. I find few people are late if you set the boundaries out clearly. Most people value their time more when they are paying for it.

Fees

Therapists seem to get jumpy around fees, particularly those who have worked in organisations or voluntarily as it is not something they have had to think about. In private practice money needs to be thought about at great length. This is where you need to put your business hat on and recognise you are running a company that needs to earn you a salary. Don't be embarrassed when talking about money with your clients or it is likely they will pick up on it. Again make it a straightforward part of your contract stating your fees and how and when you expect them to be paid.

How much do I charge

How much you are charging is up to you and not something I can tell because it varies so much. What I can share is how I came to a decision about my fees.

1. Take another look at your local competition and see how much others are charging in your area.
2. Think about your outgoings and work out what would be a healthy profit for you and then adjust your price to suit this.

3. If you come in too low you may be seen as less competent, plus you may be devaluing what you do and the skills you have to offer.

4. Take into consideration how much experience and qualifications you have; however do not be fooled into believing that just because you are less qualified than some you must charge a much lower rate.

5. In the beginning I did not offer low cost counselling as I wasn't in the right financial position. However now I have my ideal numbers I have one or two lower cost slots that I offer to people on lower incomes.

6. The final option is to have a sliding scale dependant on people's yearly salary.

The price of your sessions needs to be included in your business contract to maintain transparency.

Payment methods

There are various payment methods - cash, cheque, card or BACS transfer. With a card machine you have to pay for the handset and pay a small fee for each transaction. The bonus with using a card machine is that you can accommodate clients that need to pay on a credit card, the down side is obviously the commision you will pay.

I personally don't mind how I am paid but I do state in my contract that if by cash it needs to be at the end of each session.

If my client is paying via BACS I ask that all payments are made before our session (my BACS details are found at the bottom of my email confirmation letter). I didn't start this way but after a few weeks I found myself chasing people for money, which was frustrating and a waste of my time.

Block booking sessions

It can be helpful for some clients to pay for sessions in a block to save them having to think about the money every week. You just need to keep a record of how many session they have paid for so you don't over or under charge. It can also be handy if someone else is paying for your client's session for example a parent or family member.

Cancellation policy

Most therapists whether in private practice or an organisation have a cancellation policy. This is to protect you from having your time and services misused by others. I have it in my contract that the client needs to give me at least 48 hours notice before cancelling a session otherwise they will be charged for the session. When I go through the contract I do explain that if there are extenuating circumstances then I will review the cancellation fee.

I did and do still struggle with this as I often feel bad for charging people; however most people accept when you explain why you need to enforce the boundary and trust me it's likely they won't do it again! Remember you have room costs, time costs and you could have given that slot to another client. It might feel awkward having these conversations but go back to your written contract that they signed. It is very difficult to argue with something that is in black and white. A big part of the cancellation policy I have found is about learning to value your time and expertise, if you value yourself then others will be more likely to value you and the service you are offering.

People not paying

This is not something that I have experienced much thankfully; however it would be naive to think that it won't happen. Firstly, you need to state in your contract that failure to pay for the therapy will result in the sessions being terminated. Secondly, I state that we would talk about it if they really couldn't afford to pay. One of my clients recently was going through a really tough time financially and so for a period she paid me £10 per session. Once she was back on track she returned to pay me full price. Had we not had that conversation she may have made excuses about payments or not shown up. Again it might sound simple but talk about it with people, don't be embarrassed to ask them what is going on so it can hopefully be resolved.

Now the other dilemma would be if a client didn't pay and then just disappeared. This is tricky, I would continue to contact them every few days to remind them of the payment owed. If you have no response I would suggest you have three choices:

1. Use an online booking system for payments - this then ensures that they cannot book a session with you until they have paid.
2. Let it go and recognise that from time to time this happens in private practice.
3. Take them to a small claims court.

Some therapists I know insist on being paid before every session or the session does not happen. I do this if clients are using a BACS transfer but otherwise I trust people to pay me. Being from a person centred background I find this idea a little too formal and cold. However that is just my opinion. You can create a contract that suits you.

Unexpected endings and holidays

In my business contract I also include that the client has the right to leave therapy whenever they choose (I always encourage a proper ending but ultimately this is the client's choice). I also incorporate a sentence about me taking holidays and that I will give clients notice where I can.

Some clients can find it difficult when their therapist goes away so I always take this into consideration, but you can't get caught up with feeling responsible for your client's feelings. Remember they coped without you before and they will cope again. Creating an unhealthy reliance on you is not ethical or helpful to your clients.

Complaints procedure

It is only right and ethical that if your client has a complaint about your work they know where they can take it. This is another reason why it is so important to be registered with a reputable membership body because they keep you accountable outside of your practice. I let my clients know if it's something they feel they cannot resolve with me they are fully entitled to contact the BACP directly with their complaint.

Clinical Wills

A bit of a morbid one but it's helpful for you and your clients to know the procedure if you become very unwell or die suddenly. I have a written agreement with my supervisor that if this was to happen she would be informed by my family and be given access to my file keys and passwords. She would then make contact with each client to ensure they were properly informed. After this (with the client's consent) she would direct them to a reputable counsellor who could support them. Talk to your supervisor about your clinical will and once you have come to an agreement, formally document it and each keep a copy.

Part Two

Therapeutic contracts

This contract is shorter and although it is not generally written like the business contract the elements are just as important. As the title suggests this is much more about the client's therapeutic needs and how together you are going to meet them.

Outline your modality

Firstly, it is sensible to outline the perimeters of how you work as a therapist. In my experience most clients do not have any idea about different modalities. I keep it simple and explain that as a Person Centred counsellor I am led by the client and believe that given the right environment they hold the answers to their freedom and growth. I also explain that I am not there to diagnose and fix their problems, but to listen and explore what is going on for them. I then talk through what I have said with clients and see how it has impacted them.

Client goals for therapy

Secondly, you need to establish your client's goals and expectations for counselling and how you are going to achieve them. I often ask the client 'Now we know your goals for counselling how are we going to know when we have achieved them?' This then gives you an opportunity to explore the tangible changes they would like to see so you have a clearer idea of what their expectations are: Furthermore you can gauge if they are realistic or not. I do this in my assessment session, which we looked at in chapter five.

Open ended sessions

When starting with a new client you need to think about how you are going to work in terms of open or closed ended sessions. What I mean by this is are you going to do a block of sessions and then review, or are you going to check in with your client each week. Some therapists don't do either of these but continue until the client asks the question. I personally like to review the therapeutic contract with my clients every six weeks (if working long term) and re contract as to where we are going with the sessions.

Who sets the agenda

Another question that is worth discussing is 'who sets the agenda for what is discussed in each session?'. Again this will probably depend on your modality so just be transparent with your client about how you work.

As a Person Centred therapist I work differently with each client depending on their needs and how they like to work. Some of my clients like to have the freedom to talk and see where the wind blows them whereas others like structure and like to focus on specific subjects in each session. I have one client that likes to spend the first fifteen minutes talking about her week and then use the remaining time to focus on the subject she came to counselling for. What I am saying is you need to contract with every client, but that each client will be different and so each contract will reflect this. This is where the therapeutic contract feels more flexible than the business contract.

Contact between sessions

I was not sure where to put this subject because it seems business like but on reflection is actually more therapeutic. If you start seeing a client and you sense they may need some additional support, it may be that in your therapeutic contract you agree when and how they can contact you if things are really difficult. I experienced this with my counsellor when I was really struggling. We agreed that if I needed some extra support in the time we were apart I could text her and we would spend ten minutes on the phone free of charge, when it was convenient for her. I very rarely took her up on this offer but it was really helpful knowing it was there.

Accidental outside contact

It is also considerate to ask your client how they would like you to respond if you bump into each other outside the counselling room. This might sound petty but actually your client's confidentiality is paramount and they may not want to explain to someone they are with how they know you. It may be their choice that they don't want to acknowledge you outside the counselling room so this needs to be discussed initially together to avoid inadvertently damaging the relationship.

Additional contracts of care for specific client groups

Finally, it is worth noting that if you are working with specific client groups, such as people suffering with addictions, self harm, eating disorders or personality disorders, you may need to have an additional contract of care.

Let me explain. Having worked in the addictions field for many years I recognise that the therapy will only work if the client is in a coherent state to participate. Now most addicts when they are sober will swear to you that they would NEVER use and turn up. This however is a different story when they have used and come banging on your door or calling you drunk at 2:00am. It is ideal to write up a contract (extra to your business one) and state the expectations you have for them coming to therapy and what will happen if they break those boundaries. This is to keep you and them safe.

Another example would be someone who was in the depths of an eating disorder. You may decide to draw up an additional contract in which you only agree to see them if they are having regular contact with a doctor or having supported weigh ins of some kind. This may seem harsh; however when someone gets below a certain BMI their cognitive function will be greatly impaired. Like an inebriated person coming into therapy a severely underweight person needs to have limits so the sessions do not become counterproductive.

Writing reports for professionals

From time to time you may be asked by a client or an outside agency to write a referral letter or such like. Firstly, you must always get permission from the client otherwise you are breaking confidentiality. Secondly, I charge a fee of £20 for each report, which is often standard protocol within the private sector.

If you are unsure with any of this then please seek advice and support from your supervisor.

To some of you these extra contracts may feel daunting but you don't need to write them alone. This is an area where you can draw upon your supervisor's expertise to help and support you give the best to your clients.

Anna's Answers

- Spend time writing a business contract you are happy with.

- Remember to get your clients to read it and sign it so that you have a concrete agreement together.

- Approach your therapeutic contract recognising clients as individuals and adjust accordingly.

- Remember to review contracts where necessary so that your work can remain focused.

- Use your supervisor's expertise when creating your contracts.

Practical checklist

- ❏ Decide on my fees
- ❏ Decide on my payment methods
- ❏ Write and print my business contract
- ❏ Write additional contracts of care for particular client groups
- ❏ Write and print my clinical will.

Notes:

....
....
....
....
....
....
....
....
....
....
....
....
....
....
....
....
....
....
....
....
....
....
....
....

Support and healthy boundaries

I genuinely believe I could not have set up my business or continued to run it so successfully without other people's support. In this chapter we will explore the importance of different methods of support and creating a healthy boundaried work ethic, that will hold you in good stead for years to come.

One of the biggest reasons people become disillusioned with this profession is that they reach a place of burnout. That's why it is important to remember that we are doing challenging work and although you don't always feel it, each time you see a client you give part of yourself away that needs to be regularly replenished.

How many clients shall I take on

This question is twofold because 1. you need to have enough clients per week to reach your financial goal and 2. you need to take into account your emotional and mental capacity. Everyone is different and so for some people twenty clients a week would be acceptable, whereas for others like myself, I am content with thirteen to fifteen per week depending on what else is going on in my business. When I first started I worked out that to leave my part - time role and cover minimum costs I would need eight clients a week. This was not making me a profit but rather making it possible to live (just), so I worked towards that in the first six months of my business. Once I had achieved that I pushed on to my next target. Building a successful business does take time so don't be disheartened but rather set yourself realistic goals and keep being consistent with your marketing and promotion. It can feel monotonous, I'm not going to lie, but it is by being dogmatic that you will start to see results.

Secondly, you need to think about how many clients you can see per week without feeling constantly exhausted or managing for the first six months to then find yourself in a heap on the floor. This took me a while to figure out because I was new out of training when my biggest caseload had been four to six clients per week. Be patient with yourself. The beauty of private practice is that you can make these choices in your own way and time.

When I was on my placement I had to see four clients back to back due to room constraints, which I found really tiring and I felt the last client did not get the very best of me. Now I see maximum of five clients a day with plenty of space to write notes and digest the work. I do see clients back to back but I don't do it every day. Again everyone is different but for me five every day is just too much. There is no right or wrong amount and don't let anyone tell you otherwise. Boundaries like these are all part of your self care regime so do what is best for you and your mental and physical well-being.

As I have said above, only you will know what your limits are and you may have to test a few before you can answer that question fully. For example, I choose to work four days a week and I don't work late evening or weekends. This continues to feel right as I need to honour my weekends for me and the other things I am involved in. I have had to turn some clients away because of this but in the long run it has served me very well.

Waiting lists

When you are in the early stages of your business having a waiting list may seem a long way off, however it is good to mention this now because I believe if you work hard you will at some point need a waiting list. Surprisingly, I have found that clients are willing to wait if they feel you are the right therapist for them. Of course It does depend on what challenges they are facing, as they may feel they need immediate support in which case this is where you can make some recommendations and refer on; however if they are not in crisis then you can offer them a place on your waiting list and give them a rough time when a space will become free.

Changing working days/over accommodating clients

When I was at college one of my tutors gave me some excellent advice about the hours you work. She said "Choose your days/hours that you work and stick to them, because otherwise each client will dictate to you rather than you setting the boundaries."

When I first started out I knew exactly what she meant because clients would turn down the offered time or day and push for a time that I didn't work or had booked up with another activity. Again my advice would be don't let the fear of not having enough clients push you into this pitfall. If you do this then you will end up compromising your time and boundaries which will have a long-term detrimental effect (remember we are trying to avoid burnout here).

As humans we like structure and routine and so do your clients (even if they don't display this). What I have learnt is that if they really want to come and have therapy with you they will move *their* schedule. Think of other professions, if you book in to see your GP sometimes you have to make room in your schedule to make that happen. As long as you have offered a range of appropriate times then hand the responsibility back to the client and let them make the decision.

Out of hours

This is another area where I have learnt to be strict with myself. Once you have decided your working hours (don't forget to put them on your website and directories), keep yourself accountable about not exceeding them. In the beginning I was so driven by my fear of not 'getting clients' that if someone emailed me on a Friday night I would find myself replying. The issue with this is that you have no separation between what is your time and what is work time, before you know it work will be invading every aspect of your life.

Most clients do not expect an immediate response, particularly over the weekend. I suggest that if you get an enquiry out of hours, pause, breathe and leave responding until you are at work again. It will take some time and practice. Even now I can find myself responding to an enquiry out of hours and I have to gently remind myself they will still be there tomorrow.

Clients in crisis

This is in relation to people contacting you and it was another piece of excellent advice from my supervisor. If a potential client contacts you and the call comes through at a very late hour, or the email sounds rushed, desperate or confused it is likely that the client contacting you is in a place of crisis and so is reaching out to any one who will respond in that moment.

Potential clients like this can be tricky because they themselves may not have brilliant boundaries and if you engage with their chaos then you risk being sucked into their chaos, which will be unhelpful to you both.

I recently had a client who kept emailing me saying how he needed help 'now'. I offered him a few appointment dates and times, none of which were possible for him. After emailing some further dates he accepted one. This client then did not attend and was not contactable. He then contacted me and told me he had sent an email, which I had never received. After some consideration I decided to leave it up to him to request another appointment. A month later, he contacted me again with the same tone of crisis in his message and I still haven't seen him.

Now obviously I have great compassion for this person as they are clearly in distress; however it is my view that they are not in a place to commit to therapy or there is clearly something else going on. I could continue to spend a lot of time and energy on this client to find I never see them or if I did it would be very short-lived.

I know that chaos and crisis is something that comes with the territory of being a therapist, but my advice would be to not get sucked into their behaviour because it is likely you will come off worse.

Switching off digitally

You will know that being in a digital world has its benefits and a lot of what I have taught you has involved the internet, social media and phones. This is why it is so important that you have digital breaks where you can. I recently left my phone at my parents' house and so went two days without it. At first it was frustrating but after a while I realised how much digital culture was occupying my mind and a sense of being unchained from my device felt freeing. I generally recommend limiting your own screen time and finding other ways to rest that don't involve digital devices.

Switching off mentally

When starting in private practice you may be surprised by how difficult it can be to switch off mentally. Not only will you have your clients work to hold, you will have multiple tasks to achieve and for the most part they will all be new to you. This is also about boundaries and finding ways of parking work so it doesn't eat into your rest.

I particularly struggled with this at the beginning of my career especially when working at a drug and alcohol rehab. I was dealing with a lot of chaos, problem solving and multitasking. At the end of the day I would leave and although my body had left my mind was still there. I would think about my clients, dream about them and by the time I went to back to work in the morning it was like I hadn't actually left.

After going to supervision I realised I needed a separation point I could tie work to. So I started allowing myself time to think about work on the drive home and once I got to a certain point (a road bollard half a mile from my house) I would leave my work there only allowing myself to think about it when I picked it up in the morning. This was such a simple mental exercise but it was life changing for me because I got the separation I needed. This took a while to get used to but before long I found I no longer needed the bollard as my brain did it unconsciously.

I found this really worked for me but it might not be a good fit for you and to be honest it doesn't really matter *how* you switch your mind off, it is the the principle of being able to do so that is important, so you don't get burnt out and feel constantly overwhelmed.

Learning when to take time out

When I was building my practice I didn't have much spare money to take time off and boy did I feel the impact of this. After my first year I booked a holiday to Ibiza (the quiet part of the island I might add!) and the hope was I would have the well deserved break I longed for. This did happen but not without a fight. The first night I didn't sleep a wink and actually ended up having a full on panic attack. It was almost like I had left it too long to have a break and then when I did stop I felt exceptionally overwhelmed. It was a hard lesson to learn but it made me realise that I needed to take more regular holidays in order to stay healthy. This doesn't have to be long expensive holidays, even if it is just a long weekend that will still give you some breathing space. I now look at my diary every six weeks and book off various dates so that I know I have regular time out.

Empathy fatigue

As therapists exhibiting empathy is so intrinsic to the work we do it is easy to forget how exhausting it can be. On a daily basis we are listening, holding and processing the traumatic thoughts, feelings and behaviours of others'. Supervision can help us to restore our reserves; however it is not a substitute for taking regular time away from our profession. Over the last few years I have observed various signs and symptoms that suggest I may be suffering from empathy fatigue, so I thought I would share them with you.

1. Starting to 'care less' about my clients. The work that I would usually find interesting starts to become tedious.
2. Feeling resentful towards clients, wishing they would 'hurry up'.
3. Clock watching in sessions.
4. Feeling constantly overwhelmed.
5. Not sleeping or sleeping too much.
6. Dreading going to work.

By becoming more aware of yourself you will find it easier to spot when you may be experiencing empathy fatigue. Ways to combat this are:

1. Taking a break/holiday.
2. Taking on less clients.
3. Screening the type of work you accept to minimise complex cases.
4. Up your supervision and support.

Supervision

Having a supportive, accessible supervisor has made such a difference to my confidence levels, particularly when starting out in private practice. Whether you have been with your supervisor for all of your career or you are looking for a new one, I cannot stress how important it is to have someone who is not only knowledgeable but is also encouraging of your venture into private practice.

I say this because I have seen peers of mine stay with the same supervisor and without meaning to the dynamic of student/teacher has continued and this has undermined their confidence and decision-making as a qualified professional. Obviously, your supervisor is operating at times as a teacher but I believe it is really important that they also respect you as a fellow counselling peer.

My supervisor challenges me to take risks (calculated ones) so that I become a better practitioner and don't stay safely in my training box. When you come out of training you will realise very quickly that things are not as black and white as you were taught and a lot of the time you will find yourself in grey areas. In private practice you do not have the backup that you have in an organisation and so your supervisor is going to be your first port of call for all your clinical needs.

As this book is about setting up a private practice I am not going to go into all the different uses of supervision as that is a whole other book! What I will say is use your supervisor well and build your relationship with them so you feel able to communicate freely. If you are unsure of something then call them or make a note so you can raise it when you next go.

As well as taking individual clients, I have spoken to my supervisor about contracts, clinical wills, advertising, managing caseloads, costs and pretty much anything else that has come up in my practice. There have also been times where we have spent a large amount of the time talking about me and how I am doing because as you know, our well-being directly affects our clients.

If you come away from supervision with a sense of encouragement and the thought 'that was money well spent' then that's a great indication of a good supervisory relationship. If you come away thinking 'I'm not sure what the point of that was' then it may be time to find a new supervisor or take a look at how you are using supervision.

How much supervision

This will depend on what your ethical framework suggests. I currently have one and a half hours a month, which feels enough for me. If I have a heavier caseload then I adjust my supervision to accommodate this. Also don't forget to specify your supervision costs in your tax return as it is a necessity.

Peer supervision

Private practice can feel really lonely sometimes, which is why having a good network of therapists around you can make such a big difference to your success. As you won't be in a team I would encourage you to build your own sense of 'team'. I do this by meeting up with colleagues that I trained with once a month or so.

I would recommend an organised peer supervision where you get together and discuss your work as this can count towards your CPD and it is also a great way of getting extra supervisory support. Alternatively you can still meet with your peers on a more social level because it is still giving you an opportunity to connect. Sometimes we just go for a coffee and it is surprising how encouraged I feel about my work when I come away.

Other support networks/social media
Being in the digital age there is now much more online in the way of support. There are various closed groups that you can join on social media where qualified therapists post and comment. It is not a supervision group as you are asked not to share any client examples; however there are forums where you can ask therapy related questions.

The pros of these groups is you can get others' opinions and experiences very quickly and I know some people find the groups immensely helpful and give them a sense of a wider community. The cons which I have experienced is the groups are not often regulated very well, meaning judgemental and condescending comments are often made (ironic really considering our profession) and rarely pulled up by the admin. I have witnessed some threads become very heated and not very kind which I think is a real shame. I also found comparing myself to others on the sites which wasn't helpful for me especially when starting out.

So what I am saying is by all means join the groups and use them to your advantage but be careful of getting sucked in to unhealthy comparison and competition.

Building good relationships in the office

I work from a chiropractic clinic and a church community centre and in each of these places I have built good relationships with others. Having a community of working people around you can be extremely motivating and also provides you with that sense of team even though you are not working together. I love going in and having a cup of tea with the receptionist, or chatting through my weekend with the youth worker. It is these little touches that create a team working environment while doing a job that can be very isolating.

I have worked from home and worked in a premises and I have to admit I am much more productive when there are others around me who are working as it encourages me to focus on what I am doing. I also love that feeling of going home and knowing my work is done for the day.

If you are working from home then this is where you may have to work a little harder to create that sense of community we have been talking about.

Therapy for the therapist

As therapists we tend to love a bit of personal therapy (well I do anyway) and this is another option in terms of support, especially at the beginning of your journey into private practice. It may be that starting up private practice will push all sorts of buttons in you such as 'not being good enough', 'what if I fail' and 'I can't do this' and so it is good to be aware of where you may take some of these barriers. I have chosen to dip in and out of therapy during setting up my business and it has been helpful to have some deeper emotional support.

On a side note be aware you cannot put personal therapy through your tax return because it is not a necessity for your business - sorry guys!

Self-care habits

Now I don't want to preach to the converted as I am sure that all of you are aware of healthy self-care habits. I want to still mention it though because when starting up a private practice your business can become all consuming and a lot of good habits can slide, just when you need them the most. It is also crucial to continue these habits even when your business is stable.

Good sleep hygiene

This is obvious but so important. Getting enough sleep will mean you have more energy and motivation to get your tasks done in the day. Like children we need a consistent sleep routine, so it may be helpful to check yours. Here are some simple checks that can enhance your sleep:

1. Have a regular bedtime and waking time.

2. Have a short wind down period before bed.

3. Turn off the T.V, computers and phone half an hour before sleep (at least).

4. Have regular light tasks before bed such as giving the dog her biscuit or making your packed lunch for the next day, washing your face and brushing your teeth. These are all simple things but you are actually telling your brain you are preparing for sleep.

5. Keep gadgets out of the bedroom where you can.

6. Don't discuss with your partner or housemate emotive topics before bed but schedule a time in the day.

7. Write down tasks or reminders for tomorrow so you don't carry them to bed.

I find if I am stressed or my mind is carrying a lot my sleep will often suffer. If you are like this too then you may experience sleep issues when in the early stages of setting up your company. Don't panic your sleep will return to normal as your mind settles down. I found 'The Sleep Book' by Dr Guy Meadows (2014) extremely helpful because it includes lots of tips and tricks to help you get good restful sleep when you're struggling.

Eating well and exercise

As therapists we work in a job that is extremely sedentary. We sit for hours at a time with walking to the door to greet clients or going to the toilet our only movement throughout the day. This is why it is so important to look after our bodies through good diet and exercise. I am fortunate that I can walk to work and so I have used this time to get my steps in and process my day and the work that has been done. If this is not an option for you then maybe think about what exercise you can add into your week.

Hobbies and social life

Even when you are busy, creating space for your hobbies and social life is important. What we do can feel very heavy sometimes so having time to do things outside of work will help with balance. In the beginning I did not have much money so I had to be more inventive with the social activities I did, but it doesn't cost much to meet someone for a coffee or invite someone over for a movie and popcorn.

Whatever hobbies you love just remember to keep doing them! They are a huge outlet for your body and mind and they are a powerful tool to remain connected with who you are. I love to bake (I also love to eat) but there is something about baking that soothes me and I completely switch off all my mental chatter. Whether it's baking, cycling, running, horse riding, singing, computing or watching movies - guard your hobbies well.

A final thought on this one is to be aware that some people will often migrate to you because they know what you do for a living and before you know it you are giving a counselling session for free! Obviously, your friends and family may need support from time to time but just make sure this doesn't become a regular part of your social interaction.

Fun and down time

Remember to have fun! At the very beginning of setting up private practice everything got a little too serious and I think for a while joy seemed to vanish from my household. I am a very goal-oriented person and often forget to enjoy the process, so try and revel in the journey of building your business, keep the fun and joy alive in your daily life. Be silly, laugh and access your Free Child ego state (Berne 1950) every once in a while. Additionally don't forget to have some down time for yourself, that cup of tea away from the computer, doing a five minute meditation, having a bath or catching up on a T.V. series. It really doesn't matter how you find your down time it's just remembering to grab it with both hands.

Family time

When I get super busy this is often the first thing to go and I seem to struggle to maintain my family time. This is where the boundaries we talked about in the beginning of the chapter can come in really useful. When you are at home **be** at home. There is nothing worse than spending time with someone and feeling like they are there in body but not in spirit. Guard the days you have chosen to have off like a lion because by doing this you are not only honouring your family, you are also saying to yourself 'I am worth looking after too'. Remember work will always be waiting for you when you get back.

Anna's Answers

- Boundaries boundaries boundaries! If you want to avoid burnout you need to put healthy boundaries in place and stick to them to the best of your ability.
- Switching off mentally and digitally.
- Remembering to schedule regular breaks to avoid feeling overwhelmed.
- Hiring a supportive and experienced supervisor is crucial particularly someone who will encourage and challenge you in private practice.
- Accessing all other forms of support such as other therapists, peer supervision, social media groups and relationships in your work environment.
- Finally thinking about your self-care, forming and maintaining healthy habits in this area.

Practical checklist

- ❏ Choose my working days
- ❏ Find a supportive experienced supervisor
- ❏ Find a peer supervision group or set one up
- ❏ Join social media groups if helpful

Notes:

....
....
....
....
....
....
....
....
....
....
....
....
....
....
....
....
....
....
....
....
....
....
....
....

Chapter Eight

Maintaining success and keeping your drive

Ironically when I was writing this chapter I actually had my first experience of business becoming slow. At first I became really despondent because I felt like I was failing in some way, however after taking my feelings to supervision I had a revelation. As usual I was being extremely hard on myself and adhering to the unrealistic expectation that business remains constant, which let me tell you it does not! Secondly, instead of beating myself up I could see it as an opportunity to learn how to cope in these times and also how to combat them. This chapter will cover exactly that - how to stay motivated; how to be proactive when business goes quiet and how to continue holding onto your initial vision and hopes for the future.

Staying motivated

Staying motivated in private practice is multi-faceted because there are many different areas that you are going to need to stay on top of. This does require tenacity not only in the beginning but throughout your work life. I had never been self- employed before so I had no idea how I would handle not having an external source keeping me accountable. On reflection, money was and still is a great motivator because if I don't earn I cannot live. When you are salaried you turn up, do what you're asked and then at the end of the month you get paid. When you are self- employed you are the one that needs to generate the work. Although this can feel scary, it can also feel really empowering to be in that position.

As I explained at the very beginning of this book I wanted to be able to do something I loved and be paid for it. As you will be well aware the current climate for paid counselling jobs is poor and this is why so many are turning to private practice. I never became a therapist to become rich, I did it because it excites me and I come alive when I witness others becoming free. I adore what I do and so when I get up in the morning I don't dread going to work but wonder what the day will bring. Sure there are days where I feel tired or struggle to get going but the work always energises me and I am forever grateful for that. If you are passionate about what you do it will be at the core of your motivation - money alone is rarely enough whereas real passion has the power to drive because it is at the very core of who you are.

Something else that has helped me remain motivated is having a weekly structure. We are designed to be held by time and although sometimes it feels like a burden, having a time frame can encourage us to be proactive and productive. So my suggestion would be to think about how you would like to structure your week. Maybe get a huge piece of paper and map out your seven days. You may have things in there already that you have to work around but look at where you are going to have time for your business. This would include time for clients, admin, marketing, networking, supervision, self-care activities, blogging or vlogging and anything else you need to do to keep your business running.

Sure there will be days where it all goes to pot and your schedule is not possible but that's life! On the whole if you have a consistent routine then you will notice the difference and will avoid traps such as 'oh I'll do that tomorrow' or 'I can't be bothered to do that because it's built up and now feels overwhelming.'

Experiencing business dry spells

As mentioned above to believe that your company will never experience a dry spell is naive, so rather than hoping and praying it won't happen, accept that it is part and parcel of being self-employed. As a business you will always be looking to better your service, and generally move towards growth but it's worth bearing in mind that the journey to get there is likely to have its peaks and troughs. So how can we prepare for such eventualities? Here are some tips that I have found really helpful:

- Put away some money each month so if you hit a difficult time you will have some funds to fall back on. If this really isn't possible (it wasn't for me in the beginning) then make sure you have a good overdraft that can help you out if needed.
- Recognise that because you are the one generating your income you have the power to be proactive - this can feel really empowering.
- Get support either through supervision or talking it through with a friend, sometimes we need some help.

- Go back to basics - check your SEO and website are working to maximum capacity, publish a blog or vlog, keep a social media presence, network, enquire about EAP possibilities, send out letters to various establishments, try a different form of advertising.
- Remember you cannot be responsible for the current climate and there may be months that are just slow and this isn't your fault!
- Be patient and trust you have done all you can and things will pick up.

Don't be a one trick pony - looking for other ways to use your skills

Having more strings to your bow will mean your business is less likely to go through dry spells. Think about it, say you just do one to one counselling and then you have a period where you are not receiving enough referrals - you have nothing to fall back on whereas if you have fingers in other pies you can generate an alternative income still using your skills. As a counsellor you will have many transferable skills so utilise them. This could be running workshops in your local community; coaching others in a skill set you posses, such as mindfulness or working with bereavement; invest in some training to do couples or family work, write a book; sell your ideas - the sky really is the limit! Not only will finding other avenues in your business help with a consistent workload, it also keeps your work varied, helping you to remain fresh and current.

Not getting complacent

When business is going well it can be really easy to stop doing the things that made your company a success in the first place. This is where we can easily become complacent. When you have worked hard it can be such a relief to be in a more stable place with your private practice and by all means enjoy it, you have earned it after all! What I am saying is don't completely drop the ball. Make sure you continue marketing, networking and being open to new ideas. For example, I know that regularly posting on social media can become tedious and although you cannot see it, you are providing search engines with current and up-to-date information about your business. Don't underestimate the little things because they are acting collectively together to support your success.

Refreshing your business

Like all things in life we need to update and refresh every once in a while. Your therapy business is no different and it can also be a fun opportunity to be creative. After about two years in private practice I decided it would be good to refresh my website by changing the pictures and colours throughout and I also updated my business cards. You are not rebranding here but simply reanimating your look to keep it current.

It is also important to keep up to date with your policies and procedures making sure you are in line with current law and your code of ethics. Every once in a while I go through my paperwork to check its currency and relevance. If you do this regularly then it won't multiply into a huge job that will feel overwhelming.

Remember, this is not about change for change's sake rather an opportunity to re- group and look at what could do with refreshing. You could do this in a way that suits your learning style, as I am a visual learner I used a mind map to help me look at my business plans and where I am going.

Refreshing your training

If you are registered with a membership body, regular continued professional development will be a requirement of your code of ethics. Most bodies require around thirty hours of CPD and this can be anything from day workshops, reading, peer supervision, online courses and higher education. Although sometimes it can feel like a chore or added expense to keep training up to date, CPD is an investment in your future. It gives you the opportunity to keep up to date with current therapeutic issues, keep your academic brain ticking and most of all it ensures you give the very best to your clients. The beauty of refreshing your training is you can choose what excites you, which will make the learning much more enjoyable. As mentioned previously in this chapter, you can also use it to your advantage to further your business and add more strings to your bow.

Your vision for now and the future

This whole chapter really comes down to one thing and that is the vision for your business. The reason that companies like Apple have been so successful has not been because their products are excellent or because they have brilliant leaders (although that may be true), it is because people have captured the vision they had in the beginning. For Apple, that vision was and still is this:

"We believe that we are on the face of the earth to make great products and that's not changing. We are constantly focusing on innovating. We believe in the simple not the complex. We believe that we need to own and control the primary technologies behind the products that we make, and participate only in markets where we can make a significant contribution. We believe in saying no to thousands of projects, so that we can really focus on the few that are truly important and meaningful to us." (Apple 1976)

They sold us their vision and we bought it - the products just followed.

If you lose your vision for your therapy business you will very quickly become passive and disheartened. When business dried up briefly for me I had to go back to basics and recapture why I was doing this in the first place. Once I addressed my self-doubt and stripped away all the different layers, I kept coming back to the foundations of my vision. I want to provide a service for others that builds a culture of honour, excellence, encouragement, bringing life and significance/purpose.

My passion really is for people and I feel called to this field. That might sound really cheesy to you and that is fine because your vision may be completely different to mine, but my point is that you need to know your vision because it is what will keep you moving in this sometimes difficult but rewarding vocation. You have permission to dream, plan and think big. If I can do it, anyone can.

Anna's Answers

- Learning what keeps you motivated will ensure a thriving business.

- Dry spells will happen as a self-employed therapist, so prepare for them.

- Don't limit yourself to one way of earning an income - use your transferable skills to provide different sources of income.

- Learn not to become complacent with what you have achieved so far, but keep pushing on.

- From time to time refreshing your company's marketing, policies and procedures to keep up to date and relevant.

- Refresh your training for further opportunities now and in the future.

- Finally hold on to your original vision and think big!

Practical checklist

- ❏ Design a weekly structure
- ❏ Refresh my website
- ❏ Write down other ways I can use my skills
- ❏ Book in some CPD
- ❏ Write down my vision and my mission statement

Notes:

....
....
....
....
....
....
....
....
....
....
....
....
....
....
....
....
....
....
....
....
....

Personal Mentoring and Courses

Mentoring

Hopefully you will have now finished reading my book and feel well equipped to start on your own. However I am aware that it can be a daunting process and one where you may need that extra bit of support.

To combat this I offer a one to one mentoring service where we meet (in person or via skype) at any stage of your business set up and together make a tailor made plan for your company. I am there to mentor you and guide you through each process for as little or as long as you need. For more information about this service please contact me directly.

Courses

For many people including myself having access to interactive and visual learning is crucial. This is why the *'How to set up a successful counselling practice' two day course* is coming soon.

This will cover all the content of the book in much more depth and you will have the opportunity to bounce business ideas for your counselling practice off me and other members of the course.

It promises to be an interactive, inspiring and practical training, where I combine various methods of learning to grow your confidence in all areas of setting up your private practice.

For course details keep your eye on my website or contact me directly.

Get in touch:

- honeysettcounselling@gmail.com
- 07889026560
- www.honeysettcounselling.co.uk

References

References

Apple (1976), www.apple.com

Business Dictionary, www.businessdictionary .com

British Association for Counselling and Psychotherapy, (BACP)

Core 34, www.coreims.co.uk

Facebook, www.facebook.com

General Data Protection Regulation, (2018) www.eugdpr.org

Google my business, www.googlemybusiness.com

Godaddy, www.godaddy.com

HMRC, www.gov.uk

Health and Care Professions Council, www.hcpc-uk.co.uk

Instagram, www.instagram.com

Meadows,G,(2014).The Sleep Book Orion Publishing Co, London.

Webster.M.(1828) www.merriam-webster.com

NCS, www.nationalcounsellingsociety.org

Pinterest, www.pinterest.com

UK Council for Psychotherapists, www.psychotherapy.org.uk

vsee, www.vsee.com

Vistaprint, www.vistaprint.com

Wix, www.wix.com

123-reg, www.123-reg.com

8-10, www.8to10.com

Printed in Great Britain
by Amazon

47668120R00098